5 ways to increase your dark feminine energy

*how to be irresistible,
develop magnetic charisma,
and become the femme fatale*

by

Ella Demie

© Copyright 2023 - All rights reserved.

The content contained within this book may not be reproduced, duplicated or transmitted without direct written permission from the author or the publisher.

Under no circumstances will any blame or legal responsibility be held against the publisher, or author, for any damages, reparation, or monetary loss due to the information contained within this book, either directly or indirectly.

Legal Notice:

This book is copyright protected. It is only for personal use. You cannot amend, distribute, sell, use, quote or paraphrase any part, or the content within this book, without the consent of the author or publisher.

Disclaimer Notice:

Please note the information contained within this document is for educational and entertainment purposes only. All effort has been executed to present accurate, up to date, reliable, complete information. No warranties of any kind are declared or implied. Readers acknowledge that the author is not engaged in the rendering of legal, financial, medical or professional advice. The content within this book has been derived from various sources. Please consult a licensed professional before attempting any techniques outlined in this book.

By reading this document, the reader agrees that under no circumstances is the author responsible for any losses, direct or indirect, that are incurred as a result of the use of the information contained within this document, including, but not limited to, errors, omissions, or inaccuracies.

Table of Contents

Introduction **My Before and After** — 9

How This Book Is Organized — 17

Part 1 – **How to be Psychologically Irresistible**

Chapter 1 – **Mindsets** — 21

The Dark Feminine Energy Archetype — *21*
Accept Reality As It Is — *25*
Everything is a Game — *25*
Mental Models and Mentors — *26*
The Baader-Meinhof Phenomenon — *27*
Life is a Game of Chance — *29*
An Irresistible Personality Is Just a Set of Skills — *29*
Never Be Boring: The Importance of Having Unusual Opinions — *29*
Vulnerability as Strength — *31*
Confidence is just Competence — *33*
The List of Awesome — *35*
The Immovable Wall — *36*

Chapter 2 – **Irresistible Body Language** — 39

Why should we care about body language? — *40*
Posture — *41*
Smiling — *42*
Eyes — *43*
Tone of Voice — *46*
Touch — *47*
Sitting — *48*
Back and Neck — *49*
Hair — *49*
Walking — *50*
Emotional Reactivity — *52*

Chapter 3 – **Creating Your Reality Distortion Field**   55

- How to Master Conversations   55
- The 3 Magical Mindsets   56
- How to Have Playful, Silly, and Fun Conversations...   61
- How to Have Deeper Conversations About Your Values, Beliefs, and Life Story   67
- Storytelling   69

Chapter 4 – **Self-Awareness and Emotional Control**   83

- Journaling – How to Change Your Mood and Uncover Hidden Life Patterns   83
- Psychotherapy   90
- Intentional Discomfort Exposure Therapy   92

Part 2 – **How to be Physically Irresistible**

Chapter 5 – **Your Body is a Mind-Altering Drug**   97

- The Myth That Beauty is Subjective   98
- The Hotness Percentage   98
- The Halo Effect – Unfair Benefits of Being Beautiful   100
- Scientific Beauty Standards   103
- Waist to Hip Ratio   103
- Facial Attractiveness   133
- Breast Size   110

Conclusion   145

Thank You   147

Notes   149

Introduction
My Before and After

Over the last few years, I transformed both how I act and look, and now my life is radically different. I'm so much happier, and the new ways people react to me still feel surreal.

Growing Up

Since I was young, I knew I wasn't as pretty as other girls. I was always a bit overweight, and my face wasn't well-proportioned.

As a kid, I got praised for how smart I was and how hard I worked, but I never got any compliments about my looks.

I have a sister who was always cute and has grown up to become an extremely attractive woman. We have always been very close, but the contrast between us made me grow up with this constant feeling of not being good enough.

I spent most of my time at school feeling mostly invisible. The problem with feeling ugly is that it affects how you behave and creates a negative feedback loop.

The less attractive I felt, the shyer I became, which made me interact less with other kids and become socially awkward. The whole situation became a self-fulfilling prophecy that made me go through my teenage years and the first half of my twenties with very few friends, almost no romantic experiences, and a life mostly filled with anxiety.

Dating Life

By the end of my teenage years, I had never even kissed a boy. When I went out with my friends, guys would check them out, but not even once did I feel any of them looking at me. Their eyes would always skip me and jump to the girl next to me.

When I started college, I developed a crush on a guy and texted him, suggesting we could hang out sometime or grab a coffee together. I got no reply, and a friend told me later that he had been laughing about it with his friends. I went home earlier that day and just cried the whole afternoon.

Online dating was a waste of time; the only responses I got were from people I was not attracted to at all.

Over the years, I finally got into a few short relationships (each lasting a few months) and had a couple of one-night stands, but I never really felt sexually desired.

My breaking point

Funny enough, the moment I felt like I had to really commit to changing something wasn't particularly bad compared to my previous experiences.

One night I went out with three friends to a club, and the three of them kept getting approached and complimented. At one point, each of my friends was making out with their own guy while I sat in a corner alone, sipping my drink.

I felt so rejected that night that when I got home, I barely slept. I just drunkenly wrote and wrote about everything I was feeling, about my sad life, and what I would do to change it.

Dark feminine energy

One idea that kept popping into my mind, that I had read somewhere a few weeks before, was the idea of dark feminine energy. I didn't have a defined meaning for what it meant, but in the middle of my alcohol-fueled journaling, it became a symbol of what I was trying to achieve.

Until that point, I had been half trying to accept advice like "just be yourself," "practice radical self-acceptance," "all bodies are beautiful," and "being introverted is a superpower" (at the time, I was mixing up being introverted with being shy and anxious).

And at that moment, I decided that this would not be the game I'd be playing anymore. From now on, I would just figure out what works and do that.

Some people have drastic physical transformations; there are entire reality shows about it. So, I would do what they do.

Some people get over their shyness and go on to become famous public speakers and the life of the party anywhere they go. If they can learn it, I can learn it.

The whole time I was thinking about this, I kept remembering the Radiohead lyrics from the song Creep:

I don't care if it hurts
I wanna have control
I want a perfect body
I want a perfect soul

And this ended up defining what dark feminine energy meant for me. This was the journey I was now on.

Slowly transforming

Over the following weeks and months, I went on an obsessive deep dive into anything I could find that could be part of the solution to this puzzle.

I researched fitness, nutrition, what it means to be confident, how to become funnier, how to use exposure therapy to get rid of my anxiety, how to speak, how to move, how to have better conversations, what characteristics make someone physically attractive, what cosmetic procedures are worth it, how to get a smaller waist, better skin, and so much more.

I started going to therapy, exercising, eating right, and trying anything that showed promise and that I believed would get me closer to this ideal image I wanted to achieve.

And slowly, it started working.

My body began transforming through exercise. I lost some fat around my waist, gained some muscle in my glutes, and I got a bit of an hourglass figure for the first time in my life.

I took improv and public speaking classes that were life-changing for my social anxiety.

I read many books about how to be charismatic and connect with people, and suddenly some of my conversations started shifting from boring small talk into real, intimate moments.

This change was mind-blowing for me. I realized I had lived all my life under the unconscious assumption that I was boring and uninteresting. And in a few months, it hit me emotionally that it was just a skill. Social interactions are just another game. You practice it, and you get good at it. Some people are better players, but it's not something you have, or you don't. All this time, I just needed more practice.

I started studying what made faces attractive and why wasn't my face pretty to most people.

I finally got braces, which I had wanted for years. My parents couldn't afford it while I was growing up.

I got a rhinoplasty (nose surgery), and I learned through the surgeon that I had a recessed chin, and my face would look more balanced if I also corrected that. So, I got a chin implant.

I got a bit of filler for my almost non-existent lips, and they now look like average lips.

I started a more effective skincare routine, and my acne scars faded.

And I discovered a few studies showing that I could actually increase my breasts' size without surgery, so I tried it, and it worked. I went from an A cup to almost a C cup in around eight months.

I really just tried a lot of different stuff. And with everything combined, I ended up looking and acting like a completely new version of myself in the space of around three years.

My experience with people suddenly finding me attractive

It feels like my soul was transferred into a different reality. I still wake up sometimes and feel a bit shocked when I see myself in the mirror.

I'm still not entirely used to all of this, but essentially, I'm no longer invisible. People actually notice me now when I go out, and this loss of "anonymity" still feels weird. Both in good and bad ways.

Now when I'm outside with friends, I'm usually the first one people notice and try to talk to. I lost a few friends because of this; I think some of them used to get a boost in self-esteem by comparing themselves to me. I even had a friend admitting this to me.

I changed jobs, and the people in the new place don't know how I used to be, so they've only known this new, improved version of myself.

Everyone is super friendly, and people now invite me out all the time for drinks. I also have three coworkers interested in me romantically that have asked me out, something that had never happened before in my entire life.

When I started dating again, I just had to take a few new pictures for my Tinder profile and got an overwhelming number of matches.

I actually cried after coming back from one of these first dates. Because I had incredible, passionate sex with a man I found very attractive. I got complimented the whole night, and the date went so much smoother than anything I experienced before. A few years ago, I never saw the spark in someone's eyes except after they really got to know me. This time it was there from the start.

My social media presence was always terrible before. I wasn't photogenic, so my profile was always filled with random "artistic" pictures of objects and landscapes.

Recently, I posted half a dozen new pictures of myself, and since then, one of my previous crushes has been messaging me, complimenting how I look, and inviting me to go out with his group of friends. Sometimes I have women I barely know comment things like "You look so pretty!"

In my day-to-day life, everyone is so open; they smile so much more and often try to make small talk.

It all still feels a bit absurd. So many years suffering from loneliness, with everyone telling me that it's okay to be shy and that "I don't look so bad; I can be attractive to many people." It turns out real solutions actually existed.

This whole change in experience made me feel a lot of anger for a while. I kept thinking about how superficial everyone was. Deep down, I was still the same person. Why was everyone treating me so differently now?

But over time, I accepted that this is just how reality works. And it's not even a bad thing. I was living in an imaginary world before, hoping my version of "fairness" would come true.

The reality is that no one controls their emotions. A big part of our lives is just reacting to other people.

And if the person we're reacting to is an attractive, fun woman, our reactions will naturally be much more positive.

And this is the reason I decided to write this book. I suffered a lot for what now feels like random reasons — a random combination of genes spiraled into years of pointless emotional pain.

A few months ago, I met someone, fell in love, and I'm now in the first truly happy and healthy romantic relationship of my life.

Three weeks after we started dating, he told me he was obsessed with me. At that time, this was honestly something I had never expected to hear from someone. I was always the one becoming obsessed and falling madly in love with the men I was with! It always felt like they were settling by being with me. It feels amazing to finally be in a relationship in which we're equally obsessed with each other.

It took me a lot of trial and error to get to this point in my life. This book is the collection of techniques and ideas that have made the most difference for me. If you apply them, I genuinely believe you'll become a hotter, more irresistible version of yourself. I hope you find them useful!

How This Book Is Organized

In my mind, I like to divide how attractive we are into two categories. So, this book is divided into two parts:

Part 1 – How to be Psychologically Irresistible

Have you ever met someone that wasn't particularly beautiful, but for some reason, the way they spoke and acted made everyone feel drawn to them?

I've met a few people like this, and it has always felt like magic.

The fact that we've all encountered people with this power proves that there are specific ways we can think, speak, and behave that will make people perceive us as more attractive.

In the book's first part, we'll explore a collection of behaviors and skills that will help you achieve this effect with anyone.

This part includes the first four underused ways we can practice to increase our dark feminine energy, with a chapter dedicated to each one.

Part 2 – How to be Physically Irresistible

We all know how important physical attractiveness is. Extremely hot people live almost in a different reality than the rest of us.

Even though we'll most likely never be 10/10 millionaire models because of our appearance, I'm living proof that any improvement on the hotness scale is worth it, as just a few physical upgrades were enough to completely change how people react to me.

In this chapter, we'll explore the fifth, and, in my opinion, most effective way to increase our dark feminine energy. I'll share the unconventional tricks I discovered that helped me achieve a more attractive body.

A few of the techniques I'll talk about here are probably things you've never heard about before and might even seem unbelievable.

I've always been very skeptical, so I referenced the scientific studies that convinced me these methods actually work. This way, you don't have to take my word for it; you can read the science yourself and decide which ones are worth a try.

So, let's begin!

Part I
How to be Psychologically Irresistible

Chapter 1

Mindsets

The only true test of intelligence is if you get what you want out of life.
— Naval Ravikant

The Dark Feminine Energy Archetype

While trying to improve ourselves, having an archetype of how the ideal person we're trying to become would behave in different situations can be very helpful.

In this case, we'll be thinking about what a woman in complete control of her dark feminine energy would do.

From now on, when in doubt about how to act, you can think about this archetype and keep these traits in mind.

This is the archetype I came up with for myself. You can alter it in any way that is more aligned with your values.

When I think about this idealized person, this is what I imagine she values:

Quality Over Quantity in Relationships

She's selective with the people she spends time with. She prefers to have fewer intimate relationships instead of many shallow ones. She understands that good relationships compound over time since the longer you've known someone, the more you trust them.

She knows the importance of social connections. She doesn't believe the cliché that we're supposed to be able to be happy alone. As humans, we're social animals. Loneliness is one of the most dangerous risk factors for our health.

She actively tries to build a strong support network of family and friends. She's a collector of amazing people. If she finds someone she clicks with, she proactively nurtures the relationship. If she doesn't connect with someone, she lets them slowly fade away.

Being Memorable and Enigmatic

Her life is full of interesting experiences, but most people don't know about all of them. Revealing too much can make it seem like there's nothing about her to figure out, so she's selective about what she shares.

People are constantly being surprised by unexpected facets of her life and personality.

She knows how to use social media and word of mouth to make people think of her and want to be part of her life.

Balancing Light and Dark Feminine Energy

She cares about maintaining a balance of light and dark feminine energy, especially in long-term relationships. Her light feminine energy is expressed by her nurturing, caring, and selfless side.

She practices regular self-reflection to make sure she's expressing both energies in a healthy way.

Establishing Firm Boundaries

She understands the importance of setting clear boundaries and communicating them to others. She knows she has to put her needs first and that she isn't responsible for other people's feelings.

She recognizes when situations and relationships are not contributing to her well-being and has the emotional courage to walk away from them. She is vulnerable with the people she loves and openly asks for help when she needs it.

Uncompromising Standards

She knows her worth and won't lower her standards out of laziness. If she doesn't get the results she wants, she doesn't settle for less just because it's easier. She has an excellent work ethic and will keep trying until she achieves her original goals.

Psychological Well-Being

She invests time and effort into improving her mental health. She has a collection of habits that have been scientifically shown to improve people's happiness and protect them from depression and anxiety. She regularly studies and tries new techniques from psychology and philosophy that promote emotional tranquility and goes to therapy when she needs it.

Cultivating a Healthy and Attractive Body

She puts effort into improving her physical appearance. She understands the advantages of being attractive and how much influence it can give her.

She exercises regularly, follows a healthy diet, has a skincare routine, and does cosmetic treatments to look as good as possible.

She knows that looking her best is a lever. The amount of effort she invests into her body is multiplied, improving her life in unexpected and disproportionate ways.

Pursuing Continuous Improvement

She keeps trying to find ways to develop herself. She believes personal growth is useful because it will make her achieve her dream life faster. She is constantly exposing herself to new ideas and practicing new skills.

Healthy Sex Life

She isn't ashamed of her sexuality and enjoys sex without guilt or inhibition. She doesn't let other people's narratives define her values. She talks about sex openly and is constantly exploring new ways to express herself sexually.

Humility

She doesn't brag about her skills or accomplishments. She lets people discover them indirectly since there's much more power in that.

Independence

Finally, she knows in which areas of life it's essential to be independent. She's financially independent. She has her own collection of independently selected beliefs about reality. And she takes full responsibility for her life.

***

Whether you use my archetype or create your own, think about your life and compare it to your archetype. The goal is to, over time, get closer to this ideal.

Accept Reality As It Is

Life is mostly random. Sometimes we get lucky, sometimes we don't. Things will probably not end up like you want to just because you're a good person and you deserve it. Believing this will just lead to disappointment.

You must accept reality as it is.

You must face the fact that life isn't fair, and karma is most likely not real. Some of the kindest people in the world live lives filled with suffering. Some of the worst people live long, happy lives.

Maybe you believe in reincarnation or an afterlife where everyone gets what they deserve. But at least in this life, we know that things are not fair.

Everything is a Game

The second most important belief is to accept that you'll have to take responsibility for understanding the rules and strategies of whatever game you're trying to play.

Everything is a game. School is a game, any job is a game, dating is a game. And they all have their rules and optimal strategies.

For example:

Let's say you want to climb the corporate ladder. If you stubbornly believe that hard work and dedication alone will get you a promotion, you might be in for a rude awakening when someone less qualified but more friendly with the CEO swoops in and takes it. You didn't fully understand the rules and the best strategy to win this particular game.

So, before you play any game, research what you'll need to win.

Mental Models and Mentors

Mental models are beliefs that allow you to predict the future.

Warren Buffet, the best investor of all time, has a set of mental models that allows him to recognize and predict which companies will be successful and become more valuable. These mental models made him a billionaire.

The average investor has different mental models that are not good enough to make him a billionaire.

Modern-day scientists have a good model of how the weather works, so they can predict if it will rain or be sunny tomorrow. A century ago, they had worse models, so their predictions were wrong more often.

The best mental models are closer to the truth about how the world works. So they allow for better predictions of the future.

If you're not living your dream life right now, you have the wrong mental models. You have false beliefs about the world that make you act in sub-optimal ways.

We all have them, of course. Life is a never-ending journey of identifying and replacing them with more accurate models.

Wisdom just means having better mental models. Someone very wise can predict the outcomes of their actions accurately because their beliefs match reality more closely than someone who's not wise.

Wise people invest their time, money, and effort wisely in the things that will get them closer to their goals.

So how do we improve our mental models?

1. Through trial and error.

2. By copying someone who has proven their mental models are better than ours.

Option 2 is better. In practical terms: we find someone living the life we want and copy what they're doing.

We learn their mindsets and beliefs, watch their actions, and try our best to imitate them.

You don't need to know someone personally to learn from them. Books and courses are fantastic ways you can use to learn from someone. But, if you're able, finding someone open to sharing their experiences and offering guidance one-on-one is super helpful.

A great mentor can look at you and tell you exactly what you're doing wrong and how to do it better.

The Baader-Meinhof Phenomenon

Many self-help books and motivational speakers talk about the power of affirmations as a way to manifest anything you want. There's no scientific evidence that affirmations, the law of attraction, or any of that is real.

But they CAN work as a placebo or a way to leverage the Baader-Meinhof Phenomenon.

The Baader-Meinhof Phenomenon, also known as the Frequency Illusion or Recency Effect, happens when something you've recently learned or experienced seems to pop up everywhere.

Like when you hear about a new brand and suddenly see it everywhere, or when you're considering buying a specific car, and now it feels like every other car on the road is exactly that model.

This isn't just a coincidence. It's your brain being selective about what it pays attention to. Once you learn something new or become interested in a topic, your brain starts noticing it more often.

So, how can we make this phenomenon work for us? We can do it by constantly thinking about our goals and the steps needed to achieve them.

How to Use the Baader-Meinhof Phenomenon

1. Set a clear goal: it's easier for this to work if you know exactly what you're aiming for. Write your plans in detail so your brain has a roadmap.

2. Surround yourself with visual reminders of the goal: vision boards, quotes, images, whatever keeps your goals front and center in your mind. This helps increase your chances of noticing relevant opportunities during your daily life.

3. Study the topic regularly: Read books, articles, and blogs related to your goal. Listen to podcasts and watch videos about it.

4. Talk about your goal: Chat with friends, family, and mentors about your goals and the steps you're taking to get there. This keeps you accountable and reminds the people around you of what you're trying to achieve, making them more likely to help you or notice opportunities for you.

So, in the end, do affirmations work? Probably yes, because you're priming your brain to notice details you might otherwise not have seen and can find hidden opportunities this way.

Life is a Game of Chance

Life is a numbers game.

Whatever you're chasing - launching a business, finding the love of your life, getting your dream job, making new friends - you'll probably need ten times more effort than you initially thought.

So you want to practice intelligent persistence. Don't do the same thing repeatedly if it's not working. Try all different variations until you find something that works.

Volume negates luck.

If you do enough volume of anything, eventually, you'll get lucky. As long as the volume of whatever you're trying to do is free or cheap, you can just keep trying.

An Irresistible Personality Is Just a Set of Skills

An attractive character can unlock proverbial doors, relationships, and give you a much better life. If you develop the skills that make people love being around you, you'll never be lonely again.

Charisma is just a set of skills anyone can learn and master if they're willing to practice.

Never Be Boring: The Importance of Having Unusual Opinions

Have you ever met someone and got the feeling that you can predict all their opinions during conversation?

For most topics in life, there's a "societal consensus opinion" that everyone seems to hold as a default until they really think about the subject. So, if you ask them about it, and they never paid much attention to that subject, that's what they'll say as their opinion.

For example:

I used to hold the typical, predictable opinion that watching the news is a respectable, serious activity.

Then one day, I read the book Amusing Ourselves to Death by Neil Postman, which argued that all information could be divided into two categories:

1. Information as Entertainment

2. Practical and Actionable Information

Postman believes these are the only two reasons people consume information (although some information can be part of both categories.) He argues that the news is usually 95% Entertainment with the occasional 5% Practical.

This totally changed my opinion about the news. Do I really need to know that someone died on the other side of the country? Because it seems to me that I'm probably just using this information as entertainment. It's not like I will change my life in any way after learning this "news."

So, now, if someone asks me if I watched the news, I have this relatively unusual opinion. Of course, you don't need to agree with this opinion, but it's uncommon enough to potentially spark an interesting conversation.

Unusual opinions are inherently interesting.

I'm not saying you should try creating weird opinions about anything just to be different. But I believe exposing yourself to unconventional ideas will make you a more fascinating person.

So read more books, and watch more video essays and documentaries. While having conversations, try to find interesting angles that people might not have heard before. Play devil's advocate for a bit, even if you disagree with the point you're defending (in a lighthearted way, of course, people usually don't enjoy debates).

For example, instead of simply agreeing that the latest romantic comedy was "cute" or "funny," try to say something more unusual.

Maybe you can comment about how the film breaks new ground in showing female friendships or challenges old-school gender roles.

Maybe you can point out all the ways the main character's actions made no sense because no one would ever act that way. Those are the kind of thoughts that make everyone want to hear what you have to say.

There are entire YouTube channels where people make a living just talking about movies or books. They have millions of views because they have unusual opinions.

Vulnerability as Strength

Telling people your unusual opinions is a form of vulnerability. When you express your unique points of view, you're opening yourself up for criticism and rejection.

This is why vulnerability is a form of strength. Because you are *willing* to be criticized and rejected.

Anytime you say or do something vulnerable, you're communicating to yourself and everyone else that you value

your opinion of yourself more than other people's opinions about you.

This is a subtle point that took me a bit to grasp.

For example:

Think about a billionaire wearing sweatpants and a hoodie to an important event instead of an expensive suit.

Dressing this way is an act of vulnerability because it's different, and people will comment on it and criticize it. It also signals that they don't care that people will do that.

Their own opinion of themselves matters more than anyone else's opinion of them. And if they think wearing these clothes is cool and comfortable, this is what they'll do.

Another example:

Let's say you're hanging out in a group, and you have an unusual opinion that you're not sure how other people will react to.

You have two options, you can either say it or stay quiet.

(Of course, sometimes there are valid reasons to want to stay quiet; maybe you can't be bothered to get sucked into a political debate or something. But let's assume this is the kind of unusual opinion that wouldn't make anyone angry. Maybe everyone is talking about sports, and you believe mini golf is the best, most fun sport ever invented.)

If you decide to stay quiet (maybe because you're scared that people will think you're weird), you're implying that you care more about their opinion of you than your own opinion of yourself.

You wouldn't think twice about telling this opinion to a 10-year-old kid, for example. Because you wouldn't care what he thinks of you. What you think about yourself matters more than what a kid thinks about you, so you don't feel anxiety about expressing your weird ideas.

But, with some people, you do. Now you're thinking twice before telling them what you *really* believe.

The point I'm trying to make here is that expressing yourself in an authentic way is:

1. An act of vulnerability and courage (because you're now vulnerable to rejection)

2. A reinforcing behavior that communicates to yourself and everyone else that your opinion of yourself is more important than anyone's opinion of you.

In a counterintuitive way, being vulnerable actually signals higher social status. Because people high in social hierarchies usually don't care what others (who are lower) think of them.

So, to become irresistible, you must practice being vulnerable.

Confidence is just Competence

Confidence can seem a mystery, but its source is obvious: Confidence comes from competence.

We feel confident when we have the skills to handle the task we're doing. When we've proven to ourselves in the past that we can do it successfully.

As we become more experienced and competent in an area, our confidence grows in those situations.

For example:

Let's say you want to become confident socially. The more you study how to interact with people and practice those skills, the more competent you'll feel in social situations. If you learn how to tell stories, make people laugh, have light conversations and deep conversations, you'll start to see the patterns in how people react to you. You'll know what has worked in the past and what hasn't.

The more competent you get, the more control you'll have over your life and the more confident you'll become.

How to Develop Confidence through Competence

None of this is news to us, but it's still a good reminder of the correct way to do things:

1. Pick a Skill: Break it into smaller, achievable steps. Celebrate every win along the way.

2. Embrace the Initial Failure: Accept that failure is part of achieving competence. Be willing to look like a fool and laugh at your incompetence.

3. Seek Mentorship: As I mentioned, finding someone who's already done what you want to do and learning from their experience is the fastest way to become competent in any area.

4. Find out all the hacks and tricks: Put time and money into finding the hidden leverage points related to the skill you're trying to master. Go to workshops, take more courses, and read more books. There are always small details that only masters know that can make a huge difference when learning a particular skill.

5. Practice, Practice, Practice: To become competent at anything, you've got to practice regularly. Think about professional athletes or artists. The more time you commit to improving a skill, the more competent you'll get.

The List of Awesome

We are all already competent in many areas and have amazing life experiences that make us unique. But we've never seen it all written together in one place. So this is what I suggest you do. I call it your List of Awesome.

We'll list your achievements, interests, skills, and remarkable experiences to create it.

1. Accomplishments

Start by writing down all accomplishments you are proud of. It could be anything. Things you studied, jobs you worked, personal milestones, emotional challenges. Think about times when you felt proud and put them on the list.

2. Interests and Hobbies

Create a list of every hobby that you enjoy. Whether it's art, sports, playing video games, cooking, write them all down! Your hobbies are a vital part of what makes you "you."

3. Skills

Recognize and appreciate your own skills and talents. Make a list of everything you're good at – from technical know-how to softer skills like empathy.

4. Life Experiences

Life is full of incredible experiences that shape how we see the world. List down unforgettable moments you've lived – whether it was backpacking across Europe, meeting an inspiring person, or just funny life stories that will make someone laugh.

By the end of this exercise, you'll have a long list of all the cool and unique stuff in your life. Keep adding to the list as you live new experiences or remember old forgotten ones.

Keep this list close to your heart and pull it out whenever you need proof that you're an extraordinary person with a lot to offer.

I suggest you write it down in your phone's notes. This way, it will always be available. Read it before going on a date or to get out of a negative self-esteem spiral.

The Immovable Wall

Learning how to keep your self-worth and confidence unaffected by outside events is vital as you navigate life.

You've got to know that your value is always a perfect 100/100, regardless of outside influences or opinions.

The framing I like to use is that from now on, you have an immovable wall around your mind that can't be affected by anything.

The Immovable Wall Mindset

Picture a giant concrete wall surrounding your mind, protecting it from negativity. Your value and self-worth are inside this wall, set at 100/100.

Negativity Just Bounces Off the Wall

When you experience anything negative, like insults, rejection, or failure, these experiences can't affect your Immovable Wall.

Your self-worth stays intact, no matter what obstacles you encounter or what others say or do.

Incompatibility is Inevitable

Just because someone isn't into you doesn't mean there's something wrong with you. It just means you're not compatible.

There's no way to make everyone happy in a world filled with so many unique individuals with different tastes and opinions. Incompatibility is just part of this game.

Differentiating Constructive vs. Non-Constructive Feedback

It's crucial to know the difference between constructive and destructive criticism.

Constructive criticism includes actionable advice that you can use to improve in whatever you're trying to do. Non-constructive feedback is basically just bullying. Learn to welcome constructive feedback. Non-constructive criticism just bounces off your wall.

***

In my experience, this frame can be very effective to remain unaffected no matter what life or other people throw at you.

Set your value at 100/100 and never change it again.

Chapter 2
Irresistible Body Language

Although our body language governs the way other people perceive us, our body language also governs how we perceive ourselves and how those perceptions become reinforced through our own behavior, our interactions, and even our physiology.

— Amy Cuddy

Sometimes I walk into a room and immediately notice someone who seems to have a gravitational pull. They just seem to be the center of attention. And what's incredible is that sometimes this happens even when that person is not speaking that much.

If you think about it, there is probably someone you know who has a bit of this effect. Some people just seem to have some kind of mystical quality. The X factor. So, what's going on here?

This chapter will dissect the ingredients of this irresistible cocktail of body charisma. We'll explore posture, tonality, eye contact, and the mindsets that shape the way we engage with others.

By understanding and adopting these techniques, you'll be able to cultivate your own irresistible presence. So, get ready to transform the way you move through the world.

Why should we care about body language?

When thinking about body language, understanding what we're trying to achieve is important. Body language is precisely that, a language. While words can communicate almost everything, we use body language mainly to express emotions.

And in my opinion, the 3 primary emotions we want to show the world are comfort, confidence, and power. These are natural psychological traits that humans are attracted to.

We all like people who seem confident, comfortable, and powerful because they make us feel safe.

If someone seems to feel good about themselves and their situation, we assume they have things figured out. If they feel nervous or unhappy, our brain tells us something is wrong with them.

So comfort, confidence, and power.

How can we show these emotions?

A Note About Staying Relaxed and in the Moment

Even though first impressions are essential, if there's one main idea to keep in mind is to RELAX. Trying to focus on too many things while in the middle of interactions with people can be counter-productive.

So even though these guidelines are helpful to think about beforehand, when talking to people, if you notice you're getting too lost in your thoughts, just focus on staying relaxed, as that will be enough.

Posture

Your posture subconsciously communicates how healthy you are. Just imagine a young, fit person walking next to an old, sick person. Their bodies will move completely differently, and we evolved to pick up on those cues.

Keeping your body aligned

To have an attractive posture, alignment is crucial. I don't mean this in a mystical sense. I mean it practically and visually.

Pull your shoulders back and imagine a string running from your tailbone up through your head, gently pulling you up. This is your ideal posture.

Fluid Movement

Avoid stiff, tight movements and focus on moving smoothly.

One way to show that you feel comfortable (or at least fake it until you make it) is to position your body in a way that shows the more vulnerable parts of your body, like your palms, wrists, neck, and chest. This indicates you're at ease in your surroundings and not feeling defensive. Once again, vulnerability is strength.

For example:

Let's imagine two simple examples of how someone might enter a room to show how vital posture and movement are.

1. Person 1 comes in with tight, stiff movements, arms crossed over their chest, and eyes darting around the room.

2. Person 2 enters the room with smooth movements, arms relaxed at their sides, and vulnerable body parts showing.

Which one seems more attractive?

Smiling

A simple and common tip that is usually given to everyone, which I strongly agree with, is to smile. Smile a lot.

It's generally better to smile too much than too little.

Some people might tell you to act cool and serious. I tried that for a while, but I've seen much better results with smiling.

There are 3 specific situations in which I put conscious effort into smiling. I suggest you try to focus on them next time you're around people and see if it also makes a difference for you:

1. When you enter a room

You don't have to force a smile if you don't feel like it, but sometimes just making yourself smile for a moment can completely change the energy with which you enter a new situation.

I often don't feel like doing it, and the thought makes me groan. But then I end up laughing at myself for being silly. And that actually makes me feel genuinely more happy and positive than before.

So, try to smile when you enter a room or a new place. It will make a difference.

2. When you meet someone new

If you don't smile when you're introduced, it can seem like you're not interested or friendly. I've noticed that some people naturally smile when they meet someone, and this advice is obvious to them. But I've also seen a lot of very serious introductions, and it always makes me cringe a little bit.

Some people might intentionally act distant to try to make others want to get their approval. That's a risky strategy, and it might backfire on you.

I think it's wiser to smile when you meet someone new. It's easy and will make anyone feel more welcome and comfortable with you.

3. When having a conversation with someone.

We enjoy social conversations because they work as a spiral of positive emotions. One person says something, the other builds on it, and on and on. Smiling on purpose, even if nothing especially funny has been said, can kickstart or accelerate that spiral.

Smiling while you speak also shows you're confident and relaxed because someone nervous or threatened wouldn't be smiling.

Eyes

How you use your eyes can be the difference between looking confident or nervous.

Eye Movements to Avoid

1. Anxious Left-Right Pattern

Try to avoid making quick left-right motions with your eyes. By this, I mean the movement someone might make when they're caught doing something wrong and look around nervously.

This is a bad habit many people have when they're in public places. Especially when they don't know many people there.

They hold their drink tightly, talk to their one friend, but keep looking around everywhere as if they're looking for an escape route.

This implies they're not focused on the present moment or the person they're talking to, making them look insecure.

2. Side-Neck, Side-Eye Pattern

Another movement you want to avoid is turning your neck too much to look at something, like when you're checking someone out from the corner of your eye and don't want them to notice.

This reminds me of a squirrel or a bird that is always on the lookout for predators.

Sure, you can do this once in a while but don't overdo it.

Movements like these can make it seem like you're uncomfortable with being seen looking at what you're looking at.

Also, if you're talking to someone but keep looking around like that, they'll feel like you're not interested in what they're saying.

Being Unapologetic About What You're Paying Attention To

The better way is to use your whole body to direct your attention, not just your eyes and neck.

This means that if you're talking to someone, you face them with your body and your feet, not just your head.

And if you see something interesting over there, you turn your whole body in that direction, not just your head and your eyes.

This signals that you're comfortable with being seen looking at what you're looking at and fully engaged with whatever is happening around you.

So, try to do this more often in public places. Next time you go to a crowded place, pay attention to how people use their eyes, necks, and bodies to communicate emotion.

And try to use yours as a unit as much as possible. You can still look over your shoulder once in a while, of course, but don't make it a habit.

Breaking eye contact

Sometimes you might accidentally make eye contact with a stranger while looking around a room. And then you might feel awkward and look away quickly, usually down.

If you need to break eye contact with someone, try not to look down. Looking down can make it seem like you're submissive or shy.

You know how a dog looks when he knows he did something wrong and comes to you with his head down? It's kind of like that with humans too. You don't want to look like that when you break eye contact. If you have to, look left or right, that just shows that something else caught your attention.

But I think the best thing to do is to keep eye contact. Not as a staring contest or challenge but as a friendly gesture. You can just keep it for a second and smile.

If they smile back, that's great! You've just made a connection with a stranger. You've made them feel good about you and themselves.

If you're in a situation where you're supposed to be social, like a party or a bar, if you smile and they smile back, you can totally go up and talk to them. That can be a significant act of courage but create some of the most memorable interactions of your life.

Intentional Eye Contact

Many people avoid looking others in the eye when they pass them during day-to-day life.

But if you notice the most charismatic people, you'll see they have shamelessly intense eye contact.

So, as an exercise, and if you feel like it, next time you're walking in a busy place, for a set period of time, let's say 10 minutes, you can try to make eye contact with everyone you pass by and then smile at them and see if they smile back.

It's a bit of an unusual thing to do and a breaking of the typical social etiquette, so I don't expect you to do it regularly. But if you try it one day, it can be an excellent exposure therapy exercise to reduce social anxiety.

Tone of Voice

Different tones of voice are useful in different contexts. In regular conversations, the main idea you should remember is to avoid speaking in a boring monotone voice.

Variations in pitch, speed, and volume are essential to keep people interested in what you're saying.

Speaking in a Seductive Way

If you're on a date and want to talk in a more seductive way, you can focus on slowing down your words. Practice speaking with a breathy, relaxed voice. Studies have shown men rate high pitch voices as more attractive, so try to create the habit of keeping your voice on the higher side of your natural range.

Don't make this artificial. It's normal to use a variation of high and low tones. So sometimes, you can switch to a low pitch. But most of the time, if you want to sound seductive, you should aim to make your voice as high pitch as possible inside your natural range.

Touch

I have a friend who is a master of touch. If she meets someone new, she always gets close to the person she's talking to, smiles, makes eye contact, shakes their hand, and puts her other hand on their shoulder. She makes them feel like they're the only one in the room.

Sometimes people might feel uncomfortable at first, but she has such a warm and confident presence that everyone ends up loving her. She really knows how to make people feel important.

Now, you don't have to be exactly like this, but I bet you could touch people more often than you do. Most people are afraid of touching others too much, but they're missing out on a powerful way to create stronger connections.

Touching actually creates intimacy.

It's not just something you do after you know someone well – it's something you can do to get to know someone better. The sooner you break the physical barrier of touch, the faster you'll be able to create a deeper connection with someone.

How to Touch People Without Making It Awkward

Here are a few tips on touching:

Don't just tap someone lightly. That can be annoying or awkward. Instead, let your hand rest on them for a second or two and then take it away.

Good places to touch are:

1. The forearm, when you want to emphasize a point or show interest in what someone is saying

2. The shoulder when you want to greet them or say goodbye

3. The knee when you're sitting next to them

If you do it casually and confidently, this won't make anyone feel invaded.

For example: you can say, "Hey, we're going to go out for some drinks later today. Do you want to join us?" and touch their knee for a second. That's totally fine.

There's actually scientific evidence that touching for as little as one 40th of a second can make people feel closer and more connected. They've tested this with different kinds of touch, like handshakes, hugs, and pats on the back.

So, remember: don't tap, touch for one or two seconds, and start with these three spots: forearm, shoulder, and knee.

Sitting

If you're sitting and want to look as attractive as possible, here are a few tricks you can keep in mind:

4. Shift your weight to the front of your pelvis by leaning forward. This position makes your butt look more lifted and curvier, exaggerating your hourglass shape. If you're on a date with a guy you're interested in, leaning forward is also a way of directing your energy and attention to him, which can feel very seductive.

5. If possible, position your head so your eyes are a bit below his eye level. This will make him feel more dominant and give you a cute, innocent look.

6. You can also lower your chin slightly and look up at him through your lashes to look flirty and make your eyes look bigger.

7. Lean to one side, putting your weight on an armrest, for example. This will lower your eye level relative to his and draw attention to your hips.

Back and Neck

You don't have to worry too much about your lower back. If you're sitting, for instance, you can bend it as much as you want, as long as you keep your upper back straight.

You can also move your lower back in different directions as long as you don't compromise your upper back alignment.

This part is very unforgiving. You might feel great, but if your upper back is slouched, you will regret it when you see yourself in pictures later, for example.

So, you want to drop your shoulders back and away from your neck.

To optimize for attractiveness, you always want to keep your neck visible and elongated, even when you're looking down or sideways.

Never crunch your neck down or hide it behind your shoulders. It really doesn't look sexy. Instead, lift your neck up and tilt it slightly forward to create a relaxed and inviting look.

Hair

Some studies have shown that women with longer hair are perceived as more attractive. [1] So hairstyles that show off how long your hair is will probably be more appealing.

A good way to style your hair is to let one half fall in front of one shoulder, and the other half fall behind the other shoulder. This has the advantage of showing off your hair length and exposing your neck at the same time.

You can also play with your hair during conversation to draw attention to it.

Walking

Walking Posture

Men generally walk in a different way than women. Young people walk in a different way than old people.

Our goal is to walk in a way that expresses our healthy feminine energy. Here are some things to keep in mind:

Stand really straight. Don't slouch or hunch over. You don't have to be stiff or rigid, but you should be straight.

Your shoulders are critical while walking. Don't let them roll forward or droop down. That can make you look insecure or tired. Just relax and pull them back slightly so your upper back is straight and your chest is open.

Your chin should also be up, but not too up. You don't want to look arrogant or snobbish. Just keep it level and in the middle.

Eye Movement During Walking

Don't look at the floor when you walk.

I see that a lot. A lot of people just look at the floor when they're walking. And this contributes to their bad posture. Once again, if you look down, you look shy or ashamed. Keep your chest up and look people in the eyes.

Arms

Let your arms move along with your body, don't keep them rigid or fixed. You don't want to look like a robot with straight, stiff arms.

So just relax your arms and let them swing gently as you walk.

Of course, don't overdo it and swing your arms too wildly or forcefully. Just find a comfortable balance that suits you and your pace.

Don't worry too much about it or try to force it. It should feel easy and natural.

I usually carry a bag on my right arm, so sometimes I forget to move that arm as much as the other one. Sometimes I notice that one of my arms is straight and the other is moving, which can look odd.

So I try to remind myself to move both arms equally but naturally.

Hips

Focus on placing one foot in front of the other. Imagine following a line on the floor, and your feet are always over the line.

This will make your hips sway gently.

Don't overdo it or make it look unnatural. Just keep it simple and relaxed.

Move your arms in sync with your steps. You want your hips to sway, but not too much or too forcefully.

Many people nowadays walk with their feet too far apart and parallel to each other. And that's not flattering.

Opening your legs too much doesn't look very feminine. It's closer to how men walk, actually.

So you really want to walk lightly and over an imaginary straight line, like you're floating.

Emotional Reactivity

Expressing a lot of emotions is a big sign of vitality and health, so it's one of the things you need to practice to become more attractive.

This means happiness, surprise, sadness, whatever emotion you're feeling, doesn't matter how small, try to exaggerate your physical expressions of it.

Especially when talking to men, showing a lot of emotion on your face during conversations is one of the most powerful behaviors I've learned. This is probably because big emotional reactions happen naturally when we're very into someone.

Remember when you were a teenager and had your first big crush? You probably laughed way too hard at his jokes and listened very intensely to his every word.

Over time many of us learned to tone down these reactions and "play it cool."

Well, playing it cool is boring. We're all very, very attracted to emotions. If you go on a trip, for example, you want to be with the friend who gets excited about everything, not the one who looks neutral wherever she is.

So don't be afraid to react to what people say or do. If something is funny, laugh openly. If you're enthusiastic about a topic, show it with your gestures, words, and voice.

The more emotionally vulnerable and open you are, the more irresistible you'll be.

Chapter 3
Creating Your Reality Distortion Field

In his presence, reality is malleable.
— Bud Tribble

Some people have an uncanny ability to charm others with their words and ideas.

Steve Jobs was so famous and effective at this that people actually invented the term "Reality Distortion Field" for the effect that happened when he was talking about something.

Not many skills are as important as talking to live a good life.

How to Master Conversations

The other day, I was with a friend, and she told me she's working on being more charismatic. And one thing holding her back was that she felt like she didn't have anything interesting to say because nothing especially memorable had happened to her recently.

I hear this a lot from people. They think they must talk about what's new in their lives or the world. This is why talking to someone you haven't seen in a long time can be easy. Because a lot has changed. You're like, "Wow, we have so much to catch up on. We're going to chat for hours!"

But other times, maybe nothing much has changed, and you feel like you have nothing to share. Well, luckily, that's not true at all.

You don't need to constantly have a bunch of new stuff going on to connect with people. I'm going to tell you some practical mental models that have helped me be able to have endless conversations:

1. The 3 Magical Mindsets

2. How to Have Playful, Silly, and Fun Conversations

3. How to Have Deeper Conversations About Your Values, Beliefs, and Life Story

The 3 Magical Mindsets

There are 3 mindsets I find very useful during conversations:

Mindset 1 - Stop Censoring Yourself

Stop censoring yourself when you want to say something in a conversation. Don't hold back.

I've met so many people who have interesting, funny, engaging things to say all the time, but they don't say them. They think it's too weird, too boring, too risky, too personal.

For example:

A few months back, a friend of mine told me about a time she was at a coffee shop with a guy she had just met on a dating app, and he asked her, "So what do you do in life?"

And she, being quite an anxious person and not having been on too many dates, was just paralyzed by the question. She just kept thinking, "How do I answer that? Do I tell him about my hobbies, my passions, my dreams, my guilty pleasures?"

And she said she just mumbled something about reading books and watching shows.

I asked her, "Well, what were you thinking?"

And she said, "Well, I was thinking that's such a vague question. Like how do I even start to answer that? What if he thinks I'm boring, weird, or incompatible with him?"

And I said, "That's a good answer right there. If you had just said exactly what you said to me with a smile, he would have laughed, related to you, and asked you a more specific question.

So, for example, you could have said, "That's a hard question to answer because I like so many things, and I don't know where to start."

Maybe he would have smiled and asked you something like, "What's your favorite book, or what's the last show you binge-watched?"

What you're thinking is often okay to say out loud.

Another example is a friend who was at a dinner party with some old friends, and they were talking about religion and other controversial topics.

And she thought, "I want to say something to change the topic because no one seems to be having fun anymore. We haven't seen each other in a long time. This topic is really ruining the mood."

And so I asked her, "What if you just said that?"

And the truth is if she had just said that, people would likely have listened and moved on to something else.

You do need a bit of courage, though. Once again, saying what's on your mind is an act of vulnerability. Sometimes you'll get negative reactions. But this is very rare. In my experience, if you're blocked and don't know what to say, saying what you're thinking is almost always the correct choice (or at least the most fun choice!).

You don't have to have a perfect plan in every conversation. Just let yourself be yourself.

Mindset 2 · Conversation Seeds

The second mindset is to think of a conversation as a chance to scatter seeds everywhere.

I've loved gardening since I was young, so I imagine those little packets of seeds you can buy and plant in different spots.

And when there are more seeds, there are more possibilities for flowers to grow and bloom.

What happens in a conversation is that every word someone says has a potential number of directions you can take it in.

If someone says, "I'm a teacher," you can ask why they became a teacher, be curious about what they teach, or have a question about teaching in general.

That means there are a few conversational paths you can follow.

If they say, "I'm a teacher, and I work in a high school in San Francisco, mainly with math students."

There are even more paths there.

You could talk about all the aspects of teaching, but maybe you lived in San Francisco too. Perhaps you know something about the West Coast. Maybe you love math or had a great teacher who inspired you.

The point is the more you share about yourself, the more the other person has to respond to, and vice versa.

Sometimes people come to me and say, "I didn't know what to say next. I got stuck".

And the problem was not that they needed to constantly come up with new topics. They needed to take the ones already there and add more details so the other person had something to connect with and build on.

The details are the seeds. The more details you add, the more likely it is that some will bloom into longer, better conversations.

I always find that when people say they run out of things to say in a conversation, it's because they're actually talking about many things, but they're not going deep enough.

They usually give short, shallow answers instead of giving more background and context.

So put more out there, start scattering conversation seeds!

Mindset 3 - Be Very Expressive

You want to show your emotions with your whole body, not just your words. Use your eyes, mouth, hands, and everything to make people feel what you're saying.

Most people are not shy about showing emotions related to anger. Everyone loves to complain. But over the years, I've realized that many people have trouble expressing positive emotions (like happiness, excitement, joy) in a way others can see and feel.

They just don't do it often enough to make it natural.

It's essential you learn how to do that. And the way to learn it is to practice using your body during conversations.

Imagine if you were telling someone the story of how you met your soulmate or how you won the lottery. You can see how this would make your eyes and smile more expressive because the smile comes from within.

So just try to focus on the feelings and emotions of the stories you're telling.

That will make your eyebrows, your eyes, the corners of your eyes, and your mouth more animated and make people connect much more with your words. Which is ultimately our goal.

Using your hands

Another thing is to, over time, add hand gestures to your repertoire of unconscious movements.

Start by picking a simple one you can use in different situations and keep doing it until you notice you've started using it without thinking.

It can be something like waving your hands around when you're counting numbers or opening your arms wide when making a big point.

I think it's better to start with the big gestures first, as those are the ones that tend to catch people's attention and make them focus on what you're saying. You can then work on the small ones later.

How to Have Playful, Silly, and Fun Conversations

Being Funny

Becoming funnier is one of the most important social skills you can develop. Everyone loves being around funny people.

You don't have to become super witty with puns and wordplay. We're not trying to become stand-up comedians here.

But you can learn the easy ways, the hacks that anyone can do.

The main thing to remember is that talking to people is not like a job interview. You don't have to answer every question with 100% honest, factual, meaningful information.

You can just have fun; you can take a serious question and make a joke out of it to lighten up the mood, make someone smile, and then give them the real answer after. That's what the most charismatic people do.

Information is good and valuable, but even the most interesting topics can get boring if there's no humor in it.

Reusable Situational Jokes

Creating a personal collection of Reusable Situational Jokes is the fastest way to become funnier.

These are joke themes or patterns that you can apply to any situation.

I learn these from movies, books, other people, etc.

So, here are a few examples of Reusable Situational Jokes I use often. Not all of them will be funny all the time, and maybe some are entirely the opposite of your sense of humor, and you can't imagine yourself ever saying them.

That's totally fine. You don't have to copy them exactly (but you can if you want to). Just pick one or two that resonate with you and might make your friends chuckle, and give them a try!

Examples of Reusable Situational Jokes

1. The classic "That's what she said." It can turn anything sexual and be hilarious in the right context. A similar one is "…if you know what I mean…" added in a suggestive tone after almost anything. Or "Sounds like my first time." / "Sounds like my Saturday night."

2. Saying thanks when someone compliments anything not related to you. Your friend – "Wow, that's a beautiful sunset!" You – "Thank you."

3. After a friend tells you a long story: "You don't have to lie to make friends." (It's a bit riskier with people you just met, who might take it the wrong way, but that can also be funny)

4. Whenever someone drops something around you: "Yeah, just put that anywhere."

5. If someone forgets your name and calls you by the wrong name: "I've been called worse."

6. Whenever someone tells you a personal fact about themselves: Them – "I'm a doctor." You – "Well, nobody is perfect." Said jokingly with a smile, of course.

7. Whenever you meet someone unexpectedly in a random place: "We have to stop meeting like this. They'll start to suspect…"

8. Whenever anyone asks you an 'Or' question, you can always answer with a 'Yes' or 'No.' "Do you prefer pizza or lasagna?" "Yes."

9. After a long phone conversation, if someone asks you who you were talking to: "Oh, it was a wrong number."

10. When someone takes longer than usual to realize something obvious: "Next, we move on to shapes and colors."

11. If someone does something dumb while drunk: "I remember my first beer." It can also be used for anything accidental, for example, if someone trips on something: "I remember my first time walking."

12. Whenever someone says something is impossible or impractical: "You're not thinking 4th dimensionally."

Hopefully, these examples illustrate how you can be funny more often by having funny topics and jokes you know you can use in different situations.

And don't worry if you think this sounds too planned out because everyone does this without realizing it. Everyone repeats the same jokes that get the same reactions from people. And there's nothing wrong with that. It's literally what stand-up comedians get paid millions of dollars to do.

We all have these patterns that we fall back on, so we can try to be more intentional about them.

For example, when I watch a comedy show, I'll write down some phrases on my phone that I think are hilarious and can be applied to many scenarios.

I suggest you make your own list because it will be more meaningful to you. You don't need to have a physical document for it. What you should have is a mental collection of some funny themes.

And these don't have to be fixed. You should be adding, removing, changing, and combining them. That's the core of all humor and human creativity.

Other Methods for Becoming Funnier

You can improve your spontaneous sense of humor through practice. Here are two suggestions for how to accomplish that:

1. Expose yourself to the funniest people in the world

One thing you can do is to actively watch more comedy shows and movies.

Pay attention to how the comedians deliver their jokes and use their voice, face, body, and words to create humor.

You can also learn jokes and funny stories from them and try to retell them to your friends.

Just start by saying, "I heard this comedian tell a funny joke the other day," and then try to tell the joke. You know the joke is already funny, so this way, you can focus entirely on the delivery. This will improve your sense of rhythm and timing, making you funnier during day-to-day conversations.

2. Take Improv Classes

Another thing you can do is join an improv class.

During improv classes, you act out scenes without any preparation or script, so it can help you become more creative and spontaneous with your jokes.

It can also help you overcome your fear of messing up or looking silly, which often stops people from being funny.

Improv classes are one of the most important things I ever did to become more relaxed socially.

Remember that being funny is not just a skill but also a mindset. You have to be able to laugh at yourself, find humor in everyday things, and not take things too seriously.

How to connect with people over anything

A while back, a friend of mine was going out with a girl who was an artist.

My friend really liked her. She actively wanted to be her friend and hopefully more.

So they go out for drinks one night, and they're having a good time. They're laughing and joking and flirting. And then the artist asks her, "So, do you like abstract art?"

And my friend freezes. She doesn't know anything about abstract art. She used to draw when she was a kid but gave it up long ago.

She thinks abstract art is a bunch of nonsense. A monkey could do it. But she doesn't want to say that. She doesn't want to hurt the artist's feelings.

So, she says, "No, not really. I'm not into abstract art."

And the artist goes, "Oh." And then the conversation dies.

Later, she asked me, "What did I do wrong? How should I have acted in this situation? What should I have done to keep the conversation going?"

I told her, "Look, you don't have to like the same things as someone else to connect with them. You don't have to pretend to be someone you're not.

You just have to go deeper. You have to find something in common that matters.

When someone asks you a question like that, they're usually not really asking about the thing itself. They're asking about your passion, your curiosity.

You don't have to know everything about abstract art, jazz, politics, or whatever they're into. You just have to search your brain for something that makes you feel the same way they do. Do you like any kind of art?"

She says, "Yeah, when I was a teenager, I used to draw manga all the time. I would even write my own stories and then illustrate them."

I say, "That's it. That's what you say. You don't have to say you love abstract art. You just have to say you love art. You just have to share your story. You could say, 'You know what, I was never into abstract art, but I used to be crazy about drawing!'

She probably doesn't care if you like abstract art or not. She cares about what you feel. If you have something to say or not."

You can do this with anything.

Anything someone says can be an opportunity to connect if you go deeper.

If they say they like something, you can say you like something else that's related. If they say they hate something, you can tell them about the things you hate.

You can connect over any emotion. Happiness, sadness, anger, fear, whatever.

When someone tells you something, think about how they feel about it and how you feel about something similar.

How to Have Deeper Conversations About Your Values, Beliefs, and Life Story

Fun conversations are fun! But deep conversations are the ones that create lasting relationships. This means talking about your values and who you truly are.

To have a deeper conversation with someone, you must go beyond the surface level of facts, gossip, or events.

All those things are fun to talk about, but they don't really connect us to each other on a deeper level.

We all have different lives on the surface. We have different backgrounds, cultures, beliefs, and experiences. But if you dig deeper and understand why people do what they do and what matters to them, you can find genuine connections through that.

You want to make your values clear in everything that you say because that's how people will connect with you.

Step 1 – Know Yourself Better

You can't share your values with others if you don't know what they are.

Journaling is a helpful way to clarify your thoughts and ideas. Writing is better than just thinking because thoughts come and go, and we forget most of them. By writing, we're committing to the ideas we put down on paper (but, of course, we can change them anytime).

So start by asking and answering questions like these:

What is important to you?

Why are you on this life path? Why didn't you choose a different one?

What are the things that you have learned to let go of in life?

What motivates most of your actions? Is it honesty? Freedom? Ethics? Maximizing fun?

Step 2 – Practice Vulnerability During Conversations by Sharing What You Value

Once you know what matters to you, it can be hard to actually talk about it. But to become close with others, you must sometimes practice the emotional courage to start conversations about these topics.

For example:

Kindness is one of my core values in life. I believe being kind to myself and others is essential, even when it's hard or inconvenient.

A few months ago, I was at a party talking with people I had just met, and politics came up. I'm not into discussing politics because it often creates division and hostility.

So, I decided to sidetrack the conversation a little bit and share that point of view. I told them that I think the worst thing about politics is that it often makes people forget how to be kind to each other. And that the way you treat someone who disagrees with you or believes different things can reveal a lot about you.

I told them that I admire people who are kind even in tough situations because sometimes it's really not an easy thing to do.

In this case, pulling the conversation to this more emotional topic totally shifted the mood of our interaction. What was just a regular debate about politics became a more personal and deeper conversation, with some people even sharing intimate stories from their lives.

And this way, we connected on a deeper level. Because when you share your values and beliefs, you show people who you are and what matters to you.

Storytelling

Stories are extremely powerful tools. They reveal who we are, what we value, and what we have gone through. They help us connect with others and understand them better.

Learning how to tell good stories will make you more effective and persuasive in any situation. It will also make you a very entertaining person. If you think about the friends you have the most fun with, they are all probably really good at telling stories.

Just look at the great storytellers in history. Storytelling is such a valuable skill that writers and directors who know how to craft engaging stories can make millions of dollars. Same with marketers or stand-up comedians.

Stories are like spells. Whether you want it or not, if someone tells you a good story, you'll feel something, and you'll remember it. Sometimes forever.

A lot of human entertainment is just storytelling. Movies, shows, books, meeting friends and sharing gossip, all the sports drama, watching the news. Stories are actually one of the main ways we use to relax. Because stories create emotions in a predictable way.

Storytelling is one of the most amazing skills you can ever learn.

Stories Give Power to Ideas

Here is a story to show you the magical power of storytelling:

I've always believed that being able to handle rejection is a vital life skill. That we shouldn't take rejection too personally because, many times, it might not even be about us.

But whenever I shared this idea with others, they would nod politely, but I could tell they didn't really feel it.

Then one day, I had a story from a date that illustrated this point perfectly:

I met a guy online a while ago, and we decided to go out.

We went out for coffee, and we hit it off right away.

We had so much in common, we felt an instant connection, and we spent a wonderful afternoon exploring the city and chatting non-stop.

He was only visiting for the day and had a flight to catch the next morning, which added a touch of romance to the whole thing.

We had dinner together, and after dinner, since he hadn't made a move yet, I gathered my courage and asked him bluntly, "Can I kiss you?"

He looked uncomfortable for a moment and then said, "No... Sorry"

I felt disappointed, but I shrugged it off and changed the subject.

Maybe I had read the signs wrong, and he just enjoyed my company as a friend.

I didn't let it ruin the day for me because I'd still had a great time with him, and I was okay with hanging out as friends.

He left that night, and I never heard from him again.

Until a year later when he texted me out of the blue. I had almost forgotten about him by then.

But his message said something like, "Hey, I don't know if you remember me, but I still think about our date from a year ago. It was such an amazing day.

I've told people about it, and they all said I should contact you to explain what happened.

The reason I didn't kiss you was not because I wasn't into you.

It was because I had run out of toothpaste the night before and hadn't brushed my teeth all day. I was afraid you'd notice if we kissed.

I totally messed up that perfect moment, and it's been haunting me ever since!"

This text, and the reframing of what happened, were so unexpected that I just stood still for a minute, shocked, with a big smile on my face.

I thanked him for contacting me, we laughed about it and agreed to meet if we ever crossed paths again.

This one message changed how I saw the whole date.

What I thought was a rejection turned out to have nothing to do with me at all!

***

Now, when I tell someone not to take rejection personally, I follow it up with this story, and I can see how the idea clicks differently every time.

Since then, a few friends have called me after getting rejected to tell me that even though it hurt, they remembered my story and were able to see things from a different perspective. They were able to not blame themselves too much since you never really know what's going on in someone's mind.

That's the power of storytelling.

Stories can persuade people more than any bit of advice or fact can. They can also make you more memorable because stories stick in people's memories.

I like to think of it as mind control. You're creating emotions and planting ideas in someone's mind.

In this example, I had given the same advice to many people, but I needed the story to make people start believing it and remembering it.

How to Master the Powerful Art of Storytelling

Attention

Attention is the one thing that matters more than anything else when it comes to storytelling.

Attention is the currency of storytelling. It is what you need to earn from your audience and what you need to keep throughout your story.

Without attention, your story is worthless. No one will care about it, no matter how good it is.

The best storytellers know this.

They don't just tell stories; they create experiences. They don't just follow a linear sequence of events; they craft a journey of emotions.

How do they do that? How do they capture and maintain attention from start to finish?

Well, we can learn many techniques and strategies from them. We can use our voice, body language, humor, structure, and more to enhance our stories.

But for now, I want you to adopt this mindset: attention is the most crucial thing in storytelling. Don't tell a story unless you have a way to hook your audience. Attention is everything.

Emotion

If you want to capture people's attention, there is one thing you must do: make them feel something.

Emotion is the secret to engaging the people you're telling your story to.

You have to make it emotional somehow. Otherwise, you're just giving people dry facts and figures. And who wants to listen to that?

You need to master how to speak with passion, create emotional surprises in your story, and make people laugh.

Because attention comes from feeling something.

1. The Clickbait Introduction

Every story has a beginning, a middle, and an end.

Let's start with the beginning.

The beginning is where you grab people's attention and spark their curiosity.

You only need a few sentences for this, but they must be powerful. I like to call this the Clickbait Introduction.

You can do this in different ways:

1. You can create a mystery: "Last week I almost became a millionaire."

2. You can show excitement: "You won't believe what happened to me!"

3. You can address someone directly: "Sarah, you'll love this story!"

4. You can connect it to someone else's story: "That reminds me of…"

Anything that makes people look at you and wonder what you'll say is good for the beginning of a story.

You can literally think before telling a story, "What clickbait title would I create for this story?" And then say that to people to make them feel like they HAVE to hear your story.

Don't skip this part. Sometimes in group settings, some people just start telling their story without any introduction and then awkwardly realize after a while that nobody's listening.

This happens because they didn't do the simple first task of getting people's attention and letting them know they have something worth hearing.

So remember: the beginning is where you grab people's attention and spark their curiosity.

2. Rising Tension

The rising tension part is where things get interesting and exciting for your listeners.

The rising tension part of your story should make people feel a particular emotion and ask questions about what will happen next.

For example:

Let's compare how two people might tell the same story:

Person A:

"Yesterday, I had one of the creepiest moments of my life! I'm cleaning out my basement when I notice a weird crack in the wall.

I push on it, and it moves a bit. I realize it's actually a door disguised as part of the wall!

I push harder, and it opens with a creak. I see a staircase going down into the darkness.

I can hear someone speaking softly at the bottom and hear a faint sound of music. I'm freaking out at this point."

At this point, most people would be very into this story, asking themselves questions like: *Where does this door lead? How long has it been there? Who put it there? What is behind it? Would I have gone down or not?*

Through storytelling, Person A made their friends feel curiosity and a bit of fear.

Person B:

"Yesterday, I found an old door in my basement that's kind of connected to my neighbor's house."

Boring. This story creates almost no emotions, and most people would probably react with a polite "Oh, weird."

I've met many people who tell stories like this imaginary Person B. They just throw away the entire tension and emotion of the story.

Hopefully, you can see how much more engaging Person A's version is.

How to Create Tension in Your Stories

To tell a good story, you need to think about what emotions you want your story to create and then focus on that.

Here are 3 steps you can think about to do this:

1. Your story should have one big question that drives the plot: "What will happen in this situation?". In a way, every story is a mystery story.

You can also use smaller questions throughout to keep people interested and engaged.

2. Use the present tense as if your story is unfolding right now.

This makes it more immersive for your listeners.

Use words like "I am," "he comes," "we see." Don't just tell them how you felt afterward, but how you felt in the moment.

3. Describe details and emotions

Details make your stories more vivid and easier to imagine.

In the previous example, the details are the things like the crack in the wall, the sound of voices and music, and saying she was freaking out.

To add details, just think about your senses. Try to include details about light, colors, sounds, smells, tactile sensations, feelings, etc.

Think about when you're reading a fiction book, and the words almost disappear. Sometimes it can feel like you're watching a movie inside your mind. This is what we're trying to do by adding details.

3. The Climax

A good story is like a roller coaster ride: it has a start, a climb, and a drop.

The start is where you grab people's attention with something catchy and intriguing.

The climb is where you create suspense and curiosity with questions and details that paint the picture and set the mood.

The drop, or climax, is where everything comes together, and you surprise them with the emotional payoff of your story. This part should be a twist, a joke, a revelation, or a lesson learned.

The climax only works if you've built enough curiosity and tension before. If you jump to it too fast, it loses most of its power.

Two tips to make your stories' climax more impactful:

1. You should clearly know your story's climax before you start telling it.

2. Slow down and drag it a bit before revealing it. Pause for a few seconds.

This will usually make your climax more dramatic and funnier. You don't need to do it too long, just enough to make your friends more eager to know what will happen.

That's what makes people feel, "Wow, that was a great story!"

***

So that's how you tell a good story: start with a hook, climb with suspense, and drop with a surprise.

Inception Storytelling

There's a special kind of storytelling that can be exceptionally useful in life. I call it Inception Storytelling.

Inception Stories have all the advantages of normal storytelling with an added bonus: They create specific ideas in someone's mind.

A few chapters back, I suggested you write down your List of Awesome, which includes all your accomplishments, interests, hobbies, skills, and cool life experiences.

Ideally, whenever we meet someone new, we could just give them our list so they understand what an awesome person we are.

But, of course, that would be super weird.

So the right way to do it is to tell a story that includes things from your list as background information. This way, it's not bragging anymore; it's just the necessary context to understand the story.

If you watch any famous public speaker, you'll notice they often start their talks with a personal story that builds their credibility.

They want the audience to have a particular reaction. To trust them and admire them. They're all using Inception Stories to achieve this.

For example:

Let's say two of the items in your List of Awesome are:

1. *I speak multiple languages*
2. *I spent 1 year backpacking through Europe.*

You could just tell people this, but unless someone asked you about it directly, it could come off as bragging.

What would be a story that would indirectly tell people these two things about yourself?

Maybe you think back, and something like this happened:

"A while back, I backpacked through Europe with a friend, and we felt safe the entire trip except for one night.

I was in Spain, and these two guys were whispering in Spanish next to me about how they would try to steal our purses once we got off the bus.

They didn't know I could understand everything they were saying, so I went to the bus driver, and he called the police!"

This quick story would make people learn those 2 attractive facts about yourself without you having spoken about them directly.

And when someone heard that story, maybe later they would ask you, "Oh, you backpacked through Europe?" and then you can expand on it without feeling like you're trying to impress anyone.

Inception Stories to Have Conversations About Values

Another way to use Inception Stories is to show people what you value in life. So, they're a fantastic tool for creating deep, meaningful conversations.

If you're telling a story about quitting your job to backpack for a year, you're also indirectly showing people what you value: adventure over security or routine; exploration over comfort zone. These are things that you want people to know about you.

And if you tell that story and someone has the same values, you'll instantly connect over that.

So think about what values you want to share with people through stories, and start telling stories that reveal them.

Your Collection of Inception Stories

Take a minute and return to your List of Awesome and find a few attractive things you would want people to know about you. And then ask yourself what stories from your life show these traits and achievements.

Usually, there are moments in your life that capture those traits perfectly. Think of one of those moments and use it as the basis for your story. Try to use the story structure we learned before and ask yourself:

- **What's the clickbait introduction?** *How can I hook people with some statement and grab their attention?*
- **What's the big question of the story?** *How can I make them curious about what happens next?*
- **What is the climax of the story?**

Once you have written all that, the next time you're with someone that doesn't know this story, try telling it for the first time. I suggest you make it short; you can always add more details the next time you tell it to someone else.

If you repeat this exercise a few more times, you'll develop a collection of stories that show all your cool sides and will always be available anytime.

Being Supportive of Other People's Stories

Be supportive and interested in other people's stories.

Let everyone have their moments. Laugh with them when they make jokes. Don't think about how your story will be better or more exciting. Don't interrupt people or cut them off.

Some people start their stories by saying something like "That's nothing..." and then telling their story. Which is just rude and annoying. You never want to frame your story as a better version of someone else's story.

Exchange stories without making it a contest. Just connect with people and have fun.

***

So that's how you have deep conversations. First, by knowing yourself and having the courage to talk about your values. And second, by telling people your stories.

Once you master the skill of storytelling, you can use it to tell both light and fun or intimate and profound stories.

Chapter 4
Self-Awareness and Emotional Control

Without self-awareness we are as babies in the cradles.
— *Virginia Woolf*

Journaling – How to Change Your Mood and Uncover Hidden Life Patterns

Journaling has been a life-changing habit for me.

I started journaling when I was going through a tough breakup and felt lost and lonely.

I wrote down everything I felt without holding back or judging myself.

It was amazing how much better I felt after doing that.

I realized that journaling was something I wanted to do regularly to find clarity in my life.

Since then, I have tried many journaling techniques, questions, and exercises.

You might have heard before that journaling is good for you, but maybe you don't know how to start or what to write about.

I want to share with you the 6 journaling techniques I've collected over the years that have made the most difference for me.

1. Unfiltered Thoughts

To use this technique, you write down everything that is on your mind without filtering or editing yourself.

You can do this in two ways:

Write for a set amount of time

Write down every thought that comes to you throughout the day.

It doesn't matter if you write in a notebook or on your phone or computer.

2. Escaping Negative Spirals

Sometimes, I get stuck on something and can't stop thinking about it. Or I get too pessimistic about my life.

When that happens, I use these three exercises as a pattern interrupt, to break out of that cycle:

Imagine six impossible things

This is inspired by this quote from the book Alice in Wonderland:

"There is no use trying," said Alice; "one can't believe impossible things." "I dare say you haven't had much practice," said the Queen. "When I was your age, I always did it for half an hour a day. Why, sometimes I've believed as many as six impossible things before breakfast".

To do it, I let my imagination run wild and come up with six absurd scenarios. I just imagine things like a giraffe surfing a shark and then write down these fantastical scenes.

This works as an effective pattern interruption and helps me have some fun with my thoughts and break out of my negative emotion cycle.

How can I make someone else happy right now?

This helps me shift my attention from myself to others and think of ways to be kind or helpful.

It can be something simple like complimenting a friend or something more meaningful like donating money to a cause I care about.

What's something in my immediate environment that I have never noticed?

This helps me become more aware of my surroundings and appreciate the little things in life.

It can be the texture of a leaf, the smell of a candle, the taste of a fruit, etc.

This helps me stay present and feel grounded. It's basically mindfulness meditation mixed with writing.

3. The 5 Questions

The goal of this exercise is to help you appreciate the good, cope with the bad, and find life patterns.

These are the questions I use to do it, but you can change them to anything you find useful:

- *What made me happy and increased my energy today?*

- *What made me feel negative emotions?*
- *What did I learn?*
- *What are 10 things I'm grateful for?*
- *How did I progress toward my goals?*

I suggest you try these questions for a month and see what patterns you discover.

For me, the second question was very revealing. It made me face some issues that I had been avoiding – which, at the time, were a toxic relationship and a stressful job. Writing about them every day gave me the courage to deal with it.

4. The Two Versions of Yourself

This is useful when you want to make significant changes and improve yourself.

But be warned, this can be pretty tough. It really makes you be honest with yourself. I do this when I need a reality check.

I start by dividing a page into three sections:

1. What I did today

2. Best Version of Myself

3. Worst Version of Myself

At the end of the day, I write down everything I did that day in the first section: what I ate, who I talked to, what work I did - everything.

Then, for each thing, I assign a point for either the worst or the best version of myself.

For example, if I ate a whole pizza, that would be a point for the worst version. If I went for a walk with a friend, that would be a point for the best version.

At the end of the day, I add up all the points and see which version of myself won. I like how it clearly reveals all my good and bad habits and shows me in which direction my life is trending.

It can be a bit harsh and not very accurate - there's more to life than two versions of yourself - but if you need motivation to change and can handle some tough love, give it a try.

5. Journaling to Deal with Fear and Anxiety

This technique helps you break down big fears into smaller ones, come up with simple strategies to deal with them and avoid getting fixated on worst-case scenarios.

All you need is a piece of paper and a pen.

You divide your page into three columns:

1. Fears

2. Fixes

3. Outcome that you would bet on.

For example, let's say you're anxious about applying for a new job.

In the first column, you write down all the specific fears that are making you anxious.

For example: I'm worried I don't have enough experience; I'm afraid I won't do well in the interview; I'm worried I won't fit in, etc.

In the second column, you write down a simple strategy to deal with each fear.

It doesn't have to be perfect; it just has to help you feel more prepared.

For example: I'll update my resume and highlight my relevant skills; I'll practice some common interview questions and answers; I'll research the company culture and values.

These fixes are not meant to guarantee success or eliminate your anxiety completely; they are just there to help you realize that your fears are manageable and you have some control over them.

In the third column, you write down the outcome you would bet on, based on logic and probability.

This is to prevent you from imagining the worst-case scenario and letting it paralyze you.

For example, something that happens to me every time I fly on a plane: I always think the plane is going to crash and I'm going to die a horrible death.

But I know that this is just me being irrational and anxious. I deal with it by writing down the outcome that I would bet on: The plane will land safely, and I'll reach my destination alive and well.

The chances of a plane crash are so low that I wouldn't bet on them, so why should I let them bother me? Worrying about something terrible happening won't make it less likely to happen, so there's no point in doing that (easier said than done).

6. Journaling to Find What You Really Want

This method can help you answer one of the most important questions we have to face: what do I really want to do with my life?

It's helpful to look at your past, present, and future to find out what you want. You can do this by asking yourself three questions:

1. What did I want five years ago?

2. What do I want now?

3. What do I think I will want in five years?

These questions are like points on a graph. If you only have one point, you don't know where the line is going. But you can see the line's direction if you have two or more points. The more points you have, the clearer your direction is.

Answering these questions will show you how your wants have changed over time and where they are leading you.

A question I also find useful, even though it's a bit cliché, is: "If I knew I couldn't fail, what would I do?"

Of course, this is not a realistic question for all scenarios. No matter how hard I try, I almost certainly can't be an astronaut or play in the NBA. But I think the question is still valid. It can uncover the dreams where the thing that's stopping you is the social fear of failure.

Psychotherapy

Journaling is amazing, and it can give you a lot of insights about yourself. But, in my experience, there are certain things that you need a professional to help you with. If you feel like you have emotional problems like severe trauma, very destructive habits, or extremely low self-esteem, I strongly recommend you try psychotherapy.

I went to therapy for one year, and it changed my life. For a few reasons:

First, there is a vast amount of psychology research I had no idea existed, and I probably would never have found it unless I spent all my free time reading science studies.

If you want to build a house, you hire engineers and architects. Because they spent years learning the science and proven techniques to build houses. We feel this is true for any job, but many people don't realize how much this is also true for psychology.

Psychologists spent years learning about the common patterns of how humans behave and process emotions. And studying step-by-step systems to increase our psychological well-being. And they can help us in real-time.

So, a good psychologist will do two things for you:

1. They will know which therapy will most likely help you.

Could you have found those techniques yourself? Maybe, but it's unlikely. We didn't study this area for decades. We don't even know how much we don't know.

But let's say you were lucky and found the exact book with the right therapy to help you. Maybe you just went to one therapy session and asked the psychologist, "Which book is most likely to help me?" then you just read the book and never returned.

It still wouldn't be as good as in-person therapy. Because there are so many things about us that we can't see. So:

2. An experienced therapist can notice patterns that might be blind spots for you.

They have probably seen dozens of people with similar problems to yours, and they know the details of what works and what doesn't.

So, if you have been considering therapy but haven't taken the first steps to try it, do it now. It takes 5 minutes. Open your phone and set an appointment with a therapist close to you.

If you don't want to leave your house, online therapy has been proven to work as effectively as in-person therapy.

Intentional Discomfort Exposure Therapy

This is a form of emotional resistance training that will permanently reduce the bad emotions you feel in life.

Just like getting a flu shot can make you more resistant to the flu, intentionally exposing yourself to controlled negative experiences works similarly for your mind. And will make you more resilient to negative emotions.

This is an ancient idea from stoicism.

Thousands of years ago, Seneca, one of the most famous stoic philosophers, was the equivalent of a modern-day billionaire. Even though he could afford the most expensive and luxurious things available, every once in a while, as part of his stoic training, he would give up his comfortable lifestyle and live like a poor person. He would eat cheap food, wear rough clothes, and sleep on the floor.

He did this because he wanted to experience poverty, not just imagine it. He believed that this would make him less afraid of losing his wealth and more grateful for what he had.

I recommend you incorporate this idea into your life. At least once or twice a month, you should go out of your way to make yourself physically and emotionally uncomfortable.

This will raise your day-to-day happiness set point and give you the confidence to deal with future negative experiences.

Examples of Intentional Physical Discomfort

- *Taking a cold shower or ice bath*
- *Fasting for a day or more*
- *Running a marathon or doing a tough workout*
- *Sleeping on the floor or in a tent*

- *Hiking in the wilderness at night or going for a walk during a rainy day*
- *Taking a hot yoga class or long sauna session*

Examples of Intentional Emotional Discomfort

- *Facing a fear or phobia*
- *Approaching a stranger you find attractive and introducing yourself*
- *Being more vulnerable and honest than you've been before in a relationship*
- *Apologizing to someone you have wronged*
- *Going alone to a concert or similar event*
- *Trying to get rejected on purpose by asking someone for something unreasonable*

You get to decide what discomfort you want to deal with for your exposure therapy. Everyone is different and has different goals.

But be smart about it, of course. Don't do anything that could hurt you or make you sick. Always check with your doctor before you start any challenging exercise routine.

It's also best to expose yourself gradually to anything that causes you anxiety. Baby steps. For instance, if you are scared of high places, you could go to a climbing gym. If you are terrified of rejection, you could start by practicing small talk with a cashier.

The physical discomfort that you do will also depend on your level and skill. For some people, it might be a triathlon; for others, it might be walking around the block.

The main idea is to expose your mind and body to something that makes you feel uncomfortable. You will become a better person for it.

Today is as good as any day to start.

Part II
How to be Physically Irresistible

Chapter 5
Your Body is a Mind-Altering Drug

Even perfection has room for improvement.
— Ty Warner

One of the most mind-blowing things I realized over time is the power of a woman's body over men's brains.

This effect is so powerful that people will literally become addicted to it, to the point that they need professional help to deal with their addiction.

You can see this with men who are addicted to porn or sex. What are they really addicted to?

They're addicted to women's bodies. Seeing and touching a woman's body causes such an intense feeling that some people ruin their lives to feel it.

It's estimated that 20% to 40% of men cheat on their partners. Most times, for men, it's not emotional; people do it just for sex.

Why do they do it? Is it for the orgasm? They could get an orgasm any time they want.

They do it because our bodies work as a drug. They activate the brain's reward centers and act the same way as any other drug.

But, of course, not all bodies are equally irresistible.

The goal of this chapter is to turn your body into the most powerful and addictive version of itself possible.

The Myth That Beauty is Subjective

Recently, many people started believing that attractiveness is just a subjective thing defined by the current society's standards.

Is there some truth to that?

Yes.

Attractiveness is subjective in the sense that it only happens inside someone's brain. By that definition, it's obviously subjective.

It's also defined by society in that we have fashion and body type trends. You might be perceived as less beautiful if you differ too much from them.

But this is a small part of what makes someone attractive. And especially for women, there are a lot of very precisely defined characteristics that will consistently increase how beautiful someone is perceived as.

And this is what I'm interested in. This is where we focus our efforts.

The Hotness Percentage

Our main objective is to increase the percentage of people who find you hot. I call this our Hotness Percentage.

At any point in time, no matter how you look, there is a percentage of people that, if they see you, will think, "She's so hot."

For some women, that number is 99 out of 100 people; for others, the number is 1 out of 100.

But remember, even if only 1/100 people find you hot, 1% of 8 billion people is still 80 million people.

Even if only 1/1000 finds you hot, that would still be 8 million people.

It's theoretically always possible to find someone who will think you're incredibly attractive as long as you meet enough people.

But, of course, that's just not practical. Not only from a logistical standpoint - as statistically, those people are probably spread around the world - but maybe they're also not the type of people you'd be attracted to.

So, the goal is to increase our Hotness Percentage.

How to Become the Hottest Version of Yourself

We will do this by first identifying the traits that have been scientifically proven to be considered more attractive. And then putting effort into changing our bodies to get closer to those ideal beauty traits.

The closer we get, the more addictive our body becomes, and the higher the percentage of people that will think we're hot.

But Why Do Any of This?

At this point, you might be thinking, "Why should I even do any of this?"

Maybe you're already in a relationship, or perhaps you just don't enjoy worrying about how you look all the time.

And those are fair points.

The main benefit of maximizing your hotness is that you'll increase your chances of finding your dream life partner. Or, if you're not looking for that and just want to date casually, it will give you access to a larger pool of cool attractive people.

But even outside of dating, there are genuine benefits. As I mentioned, I've experienced the drastic advantages of becoming more attractive, and I'm here to tell you they're worth it.

The Halo Effect - Unfair Benefits of Being Beautiful

The Halo Effect is a thinking error that happens when we see someone with a positive trait and assume all their other traits are also positive. This effect is especially strong with beautiful people.

It's been scientifically proven that being physically attractive brings a lot of advantages in life.

The following list is not intended to make you feel bad if you weren't lucky enough to be born looking like a flawless goddess. I definitely wasn't.

It's meant to make you believe it's worth it to put significant effort into improving this area of your life.

Here are some things you might start experiencing as you increase the percentage of people that find you attractive:

Better Career

How you look matters a lot when you apply for a job or want to advance your career.

This is even often called lookism, which means that good-looking people have it easier than those who are not.

Harvard Business Review says that attractive people get more job interviews and offers and make more money than their less attractive co-workers.

Plus, they move up the ranks faster by getting promoted more often.

The truth is that hiring beautiful people is good for a company, as it can make it look better and more popular.

Happier Life

A team of economists from the University of Texas at Austin investigated the link between beauty and happiness.

They discovered that more attractive people tend to be happier than less attractive people, mainly because they earn higher incomes, enjoy more economic advantages and have more successful partners thanks to their beauty.

Better Social Life

The American Psychological Association also investigated how people's perceived personality and mental abilities are influenced by physical attractiveness.

They observed that attractive people experienced less loneliness, less social anxiety, more popularity, more social competence, and had more sexual experience than unattractive people.

Education Advantages

A review of studies on how students are seen in the education system showed that teachers favored attractive students over unattractive ones.

They unconsciously assumed that attractive students were more intelligent, had better academic performance, and had more social skills than less attractive students.

Also, studies done between 1960 and 1985 showed that attractive students actually got higher test grades. Researchers thought this might be a self-fulfilling prophecy, where the teacher's positive expectations for attractive students motivate them to work harder and achieve better results.

Fewer Consequences When Breaking Social Norms

A norm is an expectation that guides how we behave in different situations. A norm violation is when someone breaks the rule and acts inappropriately.

For example, talking loudly on the phone in a library would be a norm violation.

With attractive people, we excuse norm violations as accidents rather than normal behavior. Talamas and colleagues explain this as a consequence of the halo effect. Being attractive allows someone to break social norms with fewer social consequences.

***

In summary, yes, being beautiful is like winning the lottery. You just get a better life for free.

But like many things in life, these benefits are not binary. They exist on a spectrum. And we all can become more attractive and start enjoying more of them. So let's talk about how to do that.

Scientific Beauty Standards

A meta-analysis by Judith H. Langlois and colleagues - titled "Maxims or myths of beauty?" - concluded that "Contrary to conventional wisdom, there is strong agreement both within and across cultures about who is and who is not attractive."

This means some characteristics are more attractive than others, and these are the ones we are trying to acquire.

Not all of them are within our control. For the ones that are, some require little effort to get, some require a lot of effort, and some can only be achieved through cosmetic procedures (for example, braces to achieve a more attractive smile or a rhinoplasty to achieve a more attractive nose).

You don't need all of them to become more attractive. Each one you decide to improve will increase the percentage of people who find you hot.

So you can decide which ones are worth it to you, depending on your discipline, values, and financial situation.

Waist to Hip Ratio

Even though our current culture is obsessed with weight, research has shown that your BMI (Body Mass Index) doesn't have a big influence on how attractive you are.

What *does* have a big influence is your Waist to Hip Ratio (WHR).

In the study "Cross-cultural consensus for waist-hip ratio and women's attractiveness," Devendra Singh and colleagues concluded that "in each culture participants selected women with low WHR as attractive, regardless of increases or decreases in BMI."

This is so ingrained in our brains, and especially in men's brains, that even men who have been blind since birth prefer women with a low WHR. [31]

Various studies have found that men prefer images of women with WHRs of 0.7 to women with higher WHRs. [30]

Does this mean you can be overweight and still be considered extremely attractive by most people?

Yes, as long as your waist size is 70% or less than your hip size.

Women featured in Playboy magazine have always had a WHR of about 0.7. [30]

Most statues of fertility goddesses throughout history have had a WHR of 0.7 or less. Researchers analyzed the WHR of sculptures from Egypt, India, Japan, and the Greek and Roman Eras. They found that the majority had a WHR between 0.65 and 0.69. [29]

The desire to have an hourglass figure is clearly not a distortion of our current social media society, as many people like to argue, but actually something deeply rooted in our biology.

The Wrong Way to Calculate Your Waist to Hip Ratio

You can calculate your WHR by dividing your waist size by your hip size.

Most women are doing this the wrong way. What matters here is not your circumference but your 2-dimensional, straight-line measurements.

You can see why this is the case by imagining someone with a wide waist, completely aligned with her hips, who also has very developed glute muscles.

When seen from the front, her WHR would be 1 – if, for example, she had a straight-line waist measuring 20 inches and her hips also measured 20 inches. 20 / 20 = 1

But if she calculated her circumference measurements, her glute muscles would give her a much bigger "hip" size.

Does this mean she has the ideal WHR? No, because when seen from the front or back, her waist doesn't look smaller than her hips.

The Right Way to Calculate Your Waist-to-Hip Ratio

1. Take a picture of yourself from the front, naked, standing with your feet close together and your arms lifted to your sides or above your head (so you can see your waist and hips clearly)

2. Open the picture in a photo editing app and draw a straight horizontal line over your smallest waist points and another over your widest hip points.

3. Zoom in and measure both lines. The actual size doesn't matter, as what we want to know is the relative size. So, grab a ruler and zoom in on your picture until your hip line is 10 inches, for example.

4. Divide the waist measurement by the hip measurement. So, if you zoom until your hip line is 10 inches, and then you measure your waist line, and it measures 7 inches, the calculation will be 7 / 10 = 0.7

This would mean that when seen from the front, your waist is 70% of your hip size, which is our goal.

If you're already there, congratulations! It means your body is already extremely attractive to the majority of people.

If your WHR is more than 0.7, no worries, it just means this is an area you'll have to work on if you want to become more attractive this way.

I highly recommend that you try it, though. I believe this is the highest leverage thing you can do to make your body more attractive.

How to reduce your Waist to Hip Ratio

There are two ways to reduce your WHR.

You can either reduce your waist size or increase your hip size. Ideally, you do both.

How to Reduce Your Waist Size

The more straightforward way to reduce your waist size is to decrease your body fat percentage.

Since most of us accumulate fat over our waist, we'll get a thinner waist if we can remove it.

Now, I know we're all tired of diets and fighting ourselves to try to get thinner. If it was easy, no one would be overweight.

I'm not going to recommend any specific diet here.

What I'll do is give you the less-known tricks to lose fat I've used successfully and are backed by science. These are the ones that I used to drop my WHR from 0.82 to 0.68.

Volume Eating

The first concept you may or may not already be familiar with is volume eating.

What is volume eating?

Studies have shown that people tend to eat the same volume and weight of food every day, no matter what foods they're eating. [1] For Americans, the number is about 3 pounds of food a day (around 1400 g).

Different studies have experimented with modifying the number of calories in a dish without the subjects knowing, and they ended up eating the same volume and weight of food.

Since the meal had fewer calories for the same volume of food, they effortlessly ate only half the calories while feeling equally satiated. [2]

This is the power of volume eating.

The average human stomach can expand to fit around 4 cups of food (about 1 liter). Once we've filled our stomachs with any kind of food, stretch receptors will tell our brain that we're full and to stop eating.

If we fill our stomachs with calorie-dense foods, we'll gain weight. If we fill it with calorie-dilute foods, we'll lose weight. While feeling equally full and satiated.

So it doesn't really matter what type of diet you pick. If you want a thinner waist, your main goal is to eat the biggest volume of food with the lowest calories possible.

There is a lot of content online and infinite recipes you can choose from to achieve this. The subreddit r/volumeeating is one of my favorites. If you search YouTube, you'll also find many step-by-step delicious recipes with hilariously large volumes of food for a small number of calories.

My Secret, Scientific, Waist Shrinking Potion

The best evidence-based book I've ever read on how to shrink your waist is "How Not to Diet" by Dr. Michael Greger. In it, I discovered a lot of mind-blowing research I had never heard anyone talk about, showing unusual ways to lose fat.

After reading it, I decided to create a drink combining the biggest amount of hacks in one (relatively) easy-to-drink cocktail.

All the ingredients have been shown to make people lose fat and reduce waist size WITHOUT changing anything about their diets or exercise habits. It's literally a zero-effort waist-trimming drink.

Does it taste good? Not really. I've experimented with the ratios until I found a combination that I personally found easy enough to drink. But I like to think of it as a kind of magical witchcraft potion. Do witches drink their potions for the taste? Of course not; they drink it for its magical powers.

I suggest you start with my recipe and then try different combinations for yourself until you find something you can drink every day.

Ingredients and studies:

1. Hibiscus Tea – Researchers divided people into two groups. Over the course of 3 months, the placebo group lost 5 pounds (2,2 kg), while the hibiscus tea group lost 8 pounds (3,6 kg). That's 3 extra pounds of fat loss just by drinking a cup of hibiscus tea every day. [3]

2. Green Tea – Similar results to hibiscus tea, a meta-analysis found that people drinking green tea daily lose an extra 3 pounds (1,4 kg) over a 3-month period. [4]

3. Ginger – A meta-analysis concluded that ginger intake reduced weight and waist-to-hip ratio. [5]

4. Apple Cider Vinegar – During a 3-month trial, the placebo group gained weight, while the group consuming 2 tablespoons a day (30 ml) lost 5 pounds (2,2 kg). [6]

5. Yacon Syrup – This caramel-like syrup is made from the relatively unknown yacon plant. People eating 4 teaspoons of yacon syrup a day for 4 months lost over 30 pounds (13,6 kg) and reduced their waist size by 4 inches (10 cm)! [7]

6. Psyllium – Over a 6-month period, people taking Psyllium lost around 5 extra pounds (2,2 kg) and reduced their waist size by 1.5 inches (4 cm). [8]

None of these studies show life-changing fat loss (except the yacon syrup study, that one is incredible). But remember, they all worked without any type of diet change!

And if we combine them all, we'll be drinking a powerful, science-based, waist-shrinking potion every day. So here's how I do it:

Recipe

- *1 tea bag of hibiscus, or half a teaspoon (2 g) of dry hibiscus leaves*
- *¼ teaspoon (0,5 g) of matcha powder (matcha is just powdered green tea)*
- *1/2 teaspoon (1 g) of powdered ginger*
- *1 tablespoon (15 ml) of apple cider vinegar, or any other vinegar you like*

- *2 teaspoons (10 ml) of yacon syrup*
- *1 teaspoon (4 g) of Psyllium*
- *1 and a half cups (350 ml) of cold sparkling or still water*
- *Stevia to increase sweetness to taste*

Optional: You can try blending fruits with it to experiment with flavor variations, like strawberries or blueberries. I also sometimes like adding a pinch of baking soda to neutralize the acidity of the vinegar, which is good for protecting our teeth

Mix two batches before going to bed and leave in the fridge overnight. Drink two times a day (preferably using a straw to protect your teeth from the acidity), once immediately before lunch and once before dinner.

Why before lunch and dinner?

When people are asked to drink two cups of water right before a meal, they eat 20% less, an average of 100 fewer calories during that meal. [9]

So if we drink our potion right before lunch and dinner, we'll likely take advantage of another waist-slimming effect by drinking it at the right time.

Stomach Vacuums

There's an old-school exercise that bodybuilders like Arnold Schwarzenegger did religiously to reduce their waist size.

That exercise is the Stomach Vacuum.

The first time I heard about this exercise, I just dismissed it.

If you look for it online, you'll find a dozen YouTube videos showing girls who did it for a week or a month and reduced their waist by 1 or 2 inches.

The comment section of their videos is also filled with people saying it works and that they lost a couple of inches off their waist after doing it.

But I just couldn't rule out that maybe they don't know how to keep their measurements consistent. I can also "lose" a couple of inches off my waist by measuring it more sucked in.

Maybe they were all unconsciously sucking it in a bit harder in their "after" measurements. Or maybe they just ate less that week and lost some fat. Perhaps they were less bloated. And since no one has ever done a scientific experiment testing this exercise for waist size, I just dismissed it as wishful thinking.

Until I finally found someone who convinced me it was true.

I discovered a video of a male bodybuilder who did stomach vacuums for a year straight AFTER he was already lean. And he claims to have reduced his waist circumference by 6 inches (15 cm)! [10]

So that made me a believer, and I decided to start doing them daily.

I was ecstatic to find that it also worked for me! After 8 months of training, my waist circumference decreased by 3 inches! This didn't reduce my front look, straight-line waist size a lot, just a little bit.

But I still count it as a big win since now I regularly have the "flat stomach look" from all angles.

I became a bit lazier after 8 months, and now I only do them once or twice a week, but that has been enough for my waist to stay the same size.

So I strongly recommend you look for a tutorial online (it's easier to see how it's done than for me to explain over text) and start practicing stomach vacuums every day.

Abdominal Exercises You Should NOT Do

I don't recommend you do any other ab exercises except the stomach vacuum.

This is because traditional ab exercises will also inadvertently train your oblique muscles. And what happens when you train your obliques too much? They grow. And by growing, they will make your waist larger and increase your WHR.

So, my recommendation is to never train your obliques. They might be important in various sports and good for general athleticism. But they will make your WHR worse.

High Intensity Focused Electromagnetic Devices (HIFEM)

This is an absolutely amazing, game-changing technology. And since I discovered it, I've been annoyed that no one has created a cheap reliable version we can use at home.

HIFEM uses electromagnetic waves to make our muscles contract involuntarily.

I discovered this technology while watching Bryan Johnson, a self-proclaimed rejuvenation athlete. He's dedicating his life to testing all possible ways to increase health and longevity. And one of the machines he uses regularly is a HIFEM machine. In several of his videos, we can see him using it, telling us that 30 minutes of HIFEM training is equivalent to doing 20 thousand crunches.

After I learned about this, I dived into the scientific literature, and my mind was blown.

A 2019 study found that after 4 sessions of HIFEM, the participants had a 15% increase in abdominal muscle thickness and an 18% fat reduction.

This resulted in a 1.5 inch (3.8 cm) reduction in waist circumference! After only 4 sessions! [23]

Another study later achieved similar results after 8 sessions: 1.5 inches (3.9 cm) reduction in waist circumference, a 15% increase in muscle thickness, and a 17% reduction in fat. [24]

The problem now is how can we take advantage of this incredible technology.

From what I can tell, there are only two options. You can either go to a clinic and do the brand name treatment: EMSculpt. From what I read, they charge around 750 to 1000 dollars for each session, which in my opinion is a ridiculous price for something that only costs the price of electricity to run.

The only other option is to order a similar machine from China. There's a subreddit for people interested in this technology: r/emsculpt

Some people in this subreddit have ordered HIFEM machines from Aliexpress and Alibaba with varying degrees of success. Allegedly the original brand name EMSculpt machine is sold to clinics for something like 300k dollars.

You can get a HIFEM machine directly from the factories for around 1500 to 3000 dollars, with brand names like EMSlim and EMSzero.

Some people in the subreddit ordered these machines and are really happy with them, but there are also people saying that they received broken machines and it was a nightmare to get refunded.

Some say their machine is as intense as the clinic version; others say it's only half as strong. But since they can now use it unlimited times, for years, for the price of 2 training sessions at a clinic, in my opinion, this is definitely the way to go if you want to invest in this technology.

Unfortunately, unless you're rich, the only way to use this technology regularly is by betting around 2k dollars and hoping to get a working machine. I haven't ordered one yet, but I'm seriously considering it. Especially because you can also use it to increase your glute muscles' size, which we'll discuss in the next chapter.

High Intensity Focused Ultrasound (HIFU)

This non-invasive treatment uses sound waves to reduce the fat layer under the skin.

Studies have shown that it is safe and does not cause local damage such as burns or scarring or affect blood lipid or inflammatory markers.

A 2012 study confirmed that HIFU is a useful way to reduce waist circumference. After 3 weeks, the mean waist reduction was around 1 inch (2 cm). [11]

A 2010 study showed an average decrease in waist circumference of almost 2 inches (4,6 cm). [12]

Another 2010 clinical trial in Paris showed a reduction of around 1.5 inches (3,5 cm) after 2 months. [13]

So if you need to lose an extra 1 to 2 inches of fat around your waist and have the money for it, HIFU is a safe and effective way to do it.

Radiofrequency

Radiofrequency is another alternative you can use the same way as HIFU. With the added advantage that it will also reduce wrinkles, increase skin tightness, and reduce cellulite. [14]

Various studies have shown its effectiveness in reducing cellulite and waist circumference. [15] [16] [17] [18]

Radiofrequency machines can also be bought and used at home, saving you money if you plan on using them long-term.

Cryolipolysis – Also Known as CoolSculpting

I don't recommend you do cryolipolysis.

Even though studies have shown that it is generally safe and works, there is a rare complication estimated to happen in around 1% of people where the fat cells grow instead of dying. This is called Paradoxical Adipose Hyperplasia.

This happened to the supermodel Linda Evangelista and made her fall into severe depression because of the procedure.

There are also a lot of anecdotes of people losing sensation for months in the areas where they had cryolipolysis done.

Since there are so many other safer ways to reduce your waist size, my advice is: don't freeze your fat cells.

Ultrasonic Cavitation

This is one of my favorite methods to reduce my WHR because it's so effective and requires so little effort.

The reason that I prefer it to HIFU and Radiofrequency is it has been shown to be more effective than Radiofrequency, and it's much more common than HIFU. If you start researching online, you'll find a big community of people discussing their results with Ultrasonic Cavitation and what machines to buy.

Like HIFU and Radiofrequency, Ultrasonic Cavitation (UC) uses ultrasonic waves to break down fat deposits under the skin.

A 2020 study compared Ultrasonic Cavitation to Radiofrequency, finding that UC was more effective than RF at reducing WHR. In this study, using UC, the participants were able to reduce their WHR from 0.87 to 0.82! [19]

A 2015 study showed that people using UC plus dieting decreased their waist circumference by almost 3 inches (7 cm), while the control group that was only dieting only lost around 1 inch (3 cm) [20]

Another 2019 study compared diet and exercise *vs* diet, exercise, and Ultrasonic Cavitation.

The diet and exercise group decreased their WHR from 0.92 to 0.86.

But the diet and exercise + UC group decreased it from 0.92 to 0.82! [21]

Ultrasonic Cavitation is considered a safe and effective way to reduce body fat. [22]

While you can go to clinics, you can also buy your own machine and do it at home. This is the most cost-effective option if you plan on doing it regularly. You can buy UC machines for less than 100 dollars.

Low-level laser (light) therapy (LLLT)

LLLT has been used therapeutically for many years as a non-invasive treatment to improve pain, swelling, healing, and growing new tissue. Recently it started gaining popularity as a way to reduce localized fat, reduce cellulite, and even improve blood lipid levels! [25]

Meaning that it will not only reduce waist size as it can also lower your cholesterol! Subjects in a study lost around 1 inch (2,5 cm) in their waist circumference with just 8 sessions done over a month. [26]

Aminophylline creams

Aminophylline is a medication usually taken to treat asthma, but some studies found that using it topically, in a cream or gel, reduces body fat.

A 2023 systematic review of the scientific literature found that topical Aminophylline is a safe and effective alternative to surgery for people who want to reduce fat in a specific body part. [27]

The most impressive result was found in a 2007 study where people were divided into a diet group and a diet + aminophylline cream group.

The diet group reduced their waist circumference by 2 inches (5 cm), but the diet + aminophylline cream group reduced it by over 4 inches (11 cm)! [28]

Unfortunately, this is another one of those findings only known by such a small number of people that almost no one is selling it. So I haven't found a cheap aminophylline cream to try yet.

Liposuction

Liposuction is the fastest way to reduce your waist size. If you check RealSelf - a website where people post their before and after pictures of plastic surgery and surgeon reviews - 87% of people think liposuction was worth it.

Pros:

- *Immediate results*
- *You get rid of some fat cells around your waist, so if you regain weight, your waist might always look relatively smaller than the rest of your body.*

Cons:

- *Financial cost*
- *Surgery risks*
- *Pain*
- *Long recovery time*
- *Some people are left with "lumps" of fat and uneven spots*
- *Scars*
- *If you do it instead of developing good eating and exercising habits, you'll likely regain the fat*
- *Some studies show if you gain the fat back, more of it will be visceral fat, the type that is located around your organs instead of under your skin. This type of fat is associated with*

an increased risk of heart disease and diabetes, along with other chronic diseases

So is liposuction worth it?

Maybe. It's more of a bet than any of the previous methods. Some people say it's the best thing they ever done; some say it's the worst. I've never done it because I think the risks outweigh the rewards.

In the end, it's your decision and bet to make. Even if you decide to do it, take into account that the maximum amount of fat you can remove is 11 lbs (5 kg). So you need to be close to your ideal size for it to make a difference.

***

To recap, there are a lot of different strategies we can use to make our waists smaller. The healthier and most effective is, of course, just finding a way to eat fewer calories. And I still believe this should be your foundation.

But you now know a few other less-known ways to do it that can give you a massive advantage in your journey to be the hottest version of yourself.

How to Increase Your Hip Size

Increasing your hip size is more complex than decreasing your waist size since most of your hip size is determined by your bones. Some people are just lucky genetically and have naturally larger hips.

Since we can't change our bone structure, the only things we can do to increase our hip size are:

1. More muscle

2. More fat

3. Poly-L-Lactic Acid

4. Implants

Let's analyze each solution:

Increasing Hip Size – More Muscle

Resistance training is the first step, and I suggest you start incorporating it immediately and never stop.

Maintaining an exercise routine forever might seem daunting, but research has shown that the minimum effective dose is actually tiny and easy to keep doing.

We'll try to grow the Gluteus muscles, the Maximus, Medius, and Minimus (your butt muscles), and the Tensor Fasciae Latae (TFL).

The TFL muscle is a small muscle on the side of our legs. Even though it probably doesn't have a lot of potential for hypertrophy (hypertrophy just means muscle growth), it's still a muscle. As such, it can increase in size with training. And any increase will widen our hips from the front view.

Even if you have very narrow hips, bigger glutes will make you more attractive, giving you the illusion of having a smaller WHR from all side angles. Also, everyone loves a round athletic butt.

The Minimalist's Guide to Growing Your Glutes and TFL Muscles

In the research paper "Evidence Based Resistance Training Recommendations for Muscle Hypertrophy", James Fisher and colleagues reviewed all the current literature about muscle growth to provide scientific guidelines for people wanting to increase muscle size.

This is what they found. The 7 essential principles we need to follow:

1. Intensity of Effort - We should aim to contract and tire our muscles as much as possible to recruit all muscle fibers. This means exercising until the muscle physically can't lift the weight anymore.

2. Weight and Reps - We should select any weight and do repetitions until failure. They found that any weight and repetition range work equally well as long as we can reach failure.

This means you can lift a heavy weight 5 times or a lighter weight 50 times. If you do it until your muscles can't lift it anymore, both ways will induce muscle growth equally well.

3. Time Under Tension - We should always keep our muscles under tension. Unloading the muscles seems to lead to less hypertrophy.

To illustrate this, imagine you're doing hip thrusts with a barbell. If you're letting the weight rest on the floor between each rep, even if just for a second or two, you're unloading your muscles. The correct way to exercise is to never let the weight touch the ground. This way, your muscles are always under tension.

4. Number of sets – They found that one single set to failure provides similar hypertrophy to multiple sets.

A more recent meta-analysis has found that more sets produce more hypertrophy, but I still believe that the best training philosophy is to commit to only one set. Especially when we're optimizing for consistency and longevity of training.

5. Range of motion – Any range of motion works; no evidence suggests that a decreased range of motion leads to less hypertrophy.

6. Type of Resistance – We should select any type of resistance we like. Both free weights, machines, elastic bands, or body weight work equally well as long as we can reach muscular failure. Our muscles don't know where the resistance is coming from. They're either contracting or not contracting.

7. Detraining – From time to time (I suggest 2 to 4 times a year), we should take 1 to 3 weeks off and let our body rest. They found that not training for up to 3 weeks didn't lead to muscle loss and can promote greater hypertrophy once we return to training.

Now, is this optimal training?

No. This type of training gets you the most results for the least effort.

Minimalist vs. Maximalist Training

Another meta-analysis shows that doing 10 sets a week for each muscle group provides around double extra muscle gains (compared to 1 to 3 sets a week) over the same period. [1]

But the thing is, getting those extra muscle gains takes a disproportionate amount of extra effort.

Let's say you're training twice a week, doing one set to failure each day. According to the scientific literature, those two weekly sets will give you around 50% of your muscle gains.

If you trained like that for a year, let's assume you could increase your hip circumference by 2 inches.

If you did 10 sets a week, maybe in one year, you could get an increase of 4 inches. This means you would get to your goal twice as fast.

Slightly boring math ahead to prove my point. Let's compare the differences in time and effort:

Imagine you're training at home, and doing one set to failure takes you 2 minutes. Taking into account setting up the equipment, we'll say 5 minutes.

If you train twice a week, which is my recommendation, you'll be training your glutes 10 minutes a week.

Now let's calculate how much extra time it would take to do the optimal number of sets:

If you wanted to do 10 sets a week to maximize your gains, you would have to rest between sets. We'll assume 2 minutes of rest.

So one training session with 5 sets would be:

3 minutes set up + 2 minutes first set + 2 rest + 2 second set + 2 rest + 2 third set + 2 rest + 2 fourth set + 2 rest + 2 fifth set = **21 minutes total each day = 42 minutes a week.**

So you can get 50% of your gains with 2 sets, 10 minutes a week. If you want the second 50%, it will take 10 sets, 42 minutes a week. That's around 4 times more time and effort.

You have to remember, though, that there is a limit to how much you can grow your muscles. If your genetic potential is an increase of 4 inches, training with a minimalist approach might get you there in 2 years, while doing a maximalist approach would get you there in 1 year.

Is the extra speed worth the 4x effort?

It could be. It depends on your priorities. 42 minutes a week is still not that much. But the psychological difference is much more significant, I think.

Doing one hard set seems fast and easily doable.

Doing 5 hard sets sounds like a whole other thing. It's much easier to tell yourself you're too busy or tired today and skip the workout.

So I recommend committing to only 1 set to failure twice a week. If you feel like doing more after that one set, go ahead and do it. It will make you grow faster. But there's no reason to worry if you don't feel like it. You'll still grow, just slower.

The Hip Thrust

Our primary glute builder will be the Hip Thrust. You can do this with a barbell or resistance bands. You can also do it with body weight only, but our glute muscles are so strong that reaching muscular failure would take a long time. Probably hundreds of repetitions. So, for the hip thrust, weights or bands are essential.

If you have access to a gym with a hip thrust machine, this is the easiest way to train your glutes. Unfortunately, most gyms still don't have a dedicated hip thrust machine. So we're left having to find a bench with the right height, setting up the barbell, and do an uncomfortable version of the exercise.

After doing this for a few months, I discovered an exercise machine called the Booty Sprout, which allows you to do hip thrusts with resistance bands at home. I don't have any affiliation with them. I even considered trying to build my own version based on their design but concluded that buying their solution would just be easier and less expensive.

I haven't found an easier and fastest way to perform hip thrusts than the Booty Sprout. I keep it under my bed; it takes me 2 minutes to set up; I do my 1 set in 2 minutes and just push it under the bed again.

It's fast, I don't have to go to the gym to do it, and the convenience of the whole experience made me much more consistent with this exercise than I ever was before. I haven't missed a glute workout now in almost two years. Because I can always find 5 minutes twice a week.

Other Exercises

Feel free to do any other exercises you enjoy or feel might shape your body how you want. Like I said before, I like to get most of the benefits with the least amount of effort, so I only do hip thrusts. But you'll probably grow faster if you want to add other exercise variations.

Protein

The only way your muscles will grow is if you eat enough protein. Research shows that the ideal amount of protein for optimal muscle growth is at least 1.6 g for each kg of body weight.

So to calculate how much protein you should eat each day, just convert your weight to kg and multiply it by 1.6.

The way I like to make sure I get my protein is just to add as many protein shakes as necessary to reach it.

To do that, track your protein intake for a day by weighing your food and checking online how much protein you're eating. Apps like Cronometer can really help with that.

So if your protein target is 100 g a day and you're eating 50 g through your regular meals, just add a protein shake in the morning and another in the afternoon (assuming each has 25 g of protein). You'll easily reach your protein goals this way.

Creatine

Creatine is the most incredible supplement ever discovered. It's cheap, has no side effects, and research has shown tremendous benefits in various areas.

The International Society of Sports Nutrition (ISSN) considers creatine "the most effective ergogenic nutritional supplement currently available to athletes in terms of increasing high-intensity exercise capacity and lean body mass during training."

Just by taking 5 grams of creatine a day, you'll get these benefits: [2]

- *Increase in muscle mass and strength*
- *Lower cholesterol and triglycerides*
- *Reduction of liver fat*
- *Decreased risk of heart disease*
- *Antioxidant benefits*
- *Better blood sugar control*
- *Anti-cancer properties*
- *Protection against bone loss*
- *Better brain function*

Any form of creatine works, so buy the cheapest one, take 5 g daily, and never stop. It has no flavor, so you can mix it with any shake without noticing a difference.

High Intensity Focused Electromagnetic Devices (HIFEM)

As I mentioned before, I think HIFEM is a revolutionary technology. And one of the uses for HIFEM is glute training.

A 2021 study using HIFEM + Radiotherapy in the waist area, in combination with HIFEM for the glutes, found the following results:

Decreased waist circumference of around 1.5 inches (4.1 cm)

Increase in butt circumference of about half an inch (1.2 cm).

Another 2021 study found that after 4 sessions of HIFEM, glute muscle size increased by 13%! [7]

These really are mind-blowing results. For comparison, in a 2-month study where the participants did resistance training in the gym twice a week, doing 3-6 sets to failure each training day, they achieved an increase in glute size of 15%. [8]

This suggests that 4 sessions of HIFEM might be as effective at building muscle as 18 sessions of weight training!

So, if you can buy a HIFEM machine that works, you can probably replace the gym for glute training and just let the machine do the work for you.

Increasing Hip Size – More Fat

The second way to increase our hip size is to increase the amount of fat we store around our hips.

But we can't just start overeating randomly and hope it goes to our hips. Studies found that the type of fat we eat is stored in different places by our bodies.

Researchers tested this by giving the same diet to two groups of people, with the only difference being the type of fat.

The people eating saturated fat gained a significantly greater amount of body fat, with most of it going to their waists. They also built 3 times less muscle than the group eating polyunsaturated fats. [3]

This means the group eating polyunsaturated fats built more muscle and stored less fat while eating the same number of calories! The fat they stored was also distributed to other body areas instead of going mainly to the waist like in the saturated fat group.

This means that if you eat the same calories from cheese vs. avocado, the cheese will give you a worse WHR.

Where is saturated fat found?

The easiest way to notice you're eating saturated fats is to remember that saturated fats are solid at room temperature. So the fat found in foods like coconut oil, meat, cheese, and butter is the one we're trying to avoid.

Polyunsaturated fats are found in nuts, seeds, fish, and most oils. Not as tasty, I know.

So my recommendation: Slowly increase the amount of polyunsaturated fats in your diet over a few weeks while tracking your waist and hip measurements.

Do this while also eating enough protein and doing resistance training. You'll not only gain muscle but hopefully gain a little bit of fat around your hips too. Extra techniques like stomach vacuums and ultrasonic cavitation will help you maintain your waist size during this process.

Fat transfers to the hips

A quick, effective, but expensive option to increase hip size is transferring fat from other body parts to the hips.

Like other cosmetic procedures, this can give you fast and incredible results. From the natural "I'd never guess she did it" to "She doesn't look human anymore."

This is the infamous Brazilian Butt Lift (BBL). Many advise against doing it because, in 2017, the risk of death was calculated to be around 1/3000. But recently, it has come down to 1/20000 because of better techniques. [4]

For comparison, an abdominoplasty, also known as a tummy tuck, has a mortality rate of 1/13000. [5]

So a BBL is no longer the dangerous procedure it used to be. Some plastic surgeons are now even offering a rebranded "mini-bbl," basically promising that the result will look natural and not cartoonish.

If you want to take this route, it's very effective, and the results are faster and more guaranteed than the previous methods. But it will come with the same downsides I wrote about when we discussed liposuction.

If you decide to do it, research the risks and choose a certified surgeon with a good track record and good reviews on sites like RealSelf.

Poly-L-Lactic Acid (PLLA), also known as Sculptra

When people talk about fillers, they typically talk about hyaluronic acid fillers. With hyaluronic acid, the filler itself creates volume by occupying space under the skin.

PLLA works differently. It dissolves over time and stimulates the body to produce more collagen. The new collagen is then what creates the extra volume.

Collagen is essential for maintaining the skin's elasticity, firmness, and hydration and preventing wrinkles and sagging. As we age, our collagen levels decline, and that's one of the main reasons our skin loses its youthful appearance.

So PLLA is now one of the options for enhancing our hips and butts. Although the results are much more subtle than what you'd get with a fat transfer, PLLA has the advantage of being effective, minimally invasive, having almost no downtime, and being safer. [6]

PLLA is commonly used to increase volume in the "hip dip" area. So, if you search "hip dips Sculptra," you'll see the realistic results that can be achieved with PLLA.

It is an expensive option, though, because you need a lot of PLLA for the body to generate enough collagen to see a difference. The results are also not immediate. The body will gradually build collagen over the weeks following the treatment. But it might be worth it if you have the money and want to try it.

Hip Augmentation Implants

The final option to increase your hip size is hip implants. They have the advantage of being permanent and giving you more predictable results than any other methods.

There's not much more to say about that. As usual, if you decide to get hip implants, choose a surgeon with an excellent safety track record and check their patients' results to ensure it's what you want.

Facial Attractiveness

Facial attractiveness has a powerful influence on our judgments and interactions with others.

This is not something we have control over. Studies have found that attractive faces activate the reward centers in our brains. Whether we want it or not, if someone has a beautiful face, we treat them better. It has been shown that beautiful faces cause others to act with more trust, cooperation, and altruism.

Having a beautiful face is a form of power. And it's a power we can get access to.

So what makes a face attractive? And how can we make our faces more attractive? Let's find out.

A Note About Cosmetic Procedures

Unfortunately, to achieve a more attractive face, there are few options other than cosmetic procedures like braces, fillers, or surgery. If you are against doing these more invasive treatments, that is fine. You don't have to do them.

In this chapter, my goal is to provide an unbiased view of the traits that make faces beautiful and what options we have to acquire those traits.

As I mentioned before, I believe we should strive to accept reality for what it is. A more attractive face will give you a lot of advantages in life. But as with everything, there's a "risk and price *vs.* reward" analysis that each of us has to do to decide which treatments are worth it.

Teeth

Studies have shown that the smile has a massive impact on attractiveness and how people perceive your personality. [1]

Braces

If you don't already have straight teeth, the first thing you have to do is get braces. Braces will have the biggest impact on your facial attractiveness out of almost anything.

I suggest you check the top posts of all time in the r/braces subreddit to see what a difference it can make.

Teeth Whitening

Interestingly, whiter teeth don't seem to be perceived as more attractive. [2] Researchers found that teeth color doesn't influence attractiveness (Within the normal range, of course. If someone has very dark teeth, it will definitely not look good).

Bonus Tip: How to Avoid Caries and Sensitive Teeth

Almost all toothpastes contain fluoride, which has been shown to reduce caries. But bigger concentrations of fluoride work even better. Usually, toothpastes contain fluoride in a concentration of around 1500 ppm. A systematic review concluded that by using toothpaste with 5000 ppm of fluoride, you can get the following benefits: [3]

- *Enhance remineralization*
- *Lower caries risk*
- *Prevent root caries susceptibility*
- *Avoid mineral loss*

This was initially recommended to me by a friend who is a dentist and always uses toothpaste with 5000 ppm. I started using it 2 years ago and haven't had a cavity since then (the year before I started using it, I had to have two cavities treated).

To use toothpaste correctly, spit out the excess after brushing, but don't rinse your mouth with water. You need to let the fluoride stay in contact with your teeth to get the benefits.

The fix for sensitive teeth is a substance called Novamin. An overview of the clinical evidence found it effective at reducing teeth sensitivity. [4]

I've also experienced this firsthand. After I started using toothpaste with Novamin, my sensitivity to cold literally disappeared in 3 weeks. I can now eat and drink anything cold without any pain.

Chin and Jaw Alignment

The chin and jaw are the most underrated areas that can be changed to increase attractiveness.

A 2021 study found that the chin was the number 1 trait correlated with beauty when people rated faces for attractiveness. [5]

To see how vital the chin is, check the top posts in the subreddit r/jawsurgery

A 2017 study confirmed how important the lateral view of the chin is for facial attractiveness. [6]

Another 2012 study concluded that if someone's chin is recessed or protruded up to 4 mm, it doesn't impact attractiveness, but a protrusion of more than 6 mm or a retrusion of more than 10 mm was already unattractive enough to require surgery. [7]

You might be a good candidate for jaw surgery if you think you have protrusion or retrusion of your jaw. The results can be life-changing.

If your chin is just slightly retruded, you can probably improve your beauty through chin filler, fat transfer to the chin, or a chin implant.

Nose

A 2018 study discovered that 65% of people find smaller noses more attractive in women. [8]

A 2021 study compared how people are perceived before and after a rhinoplasty and found that after the procedure, the women were perceived as more attractive, sociable, feminine, confident, likable, trustworthy, and intelligent. [9]

That's a long list of benefits just from a different nose shape.

If you have a crooked or disproportionately sized nose for your face, you might be able to upgrade your attractiveness with a rhinoplasty and enjoy all its proven benefits.

Lips

Red lips are perceived as more attractive, so using lipstick increases attractiveness. [10]

An option if you don't want to constantly worry about applying lipstick is a lip blush tattoo. This is essentially a light tattoo on your lips that will last a few years. I had this done, and I've been very happy with the result. If you choose a natural color, no one will be able to notice, and your lips will just always look good, even in the morning after waking up.

Lip fullness is a less clear topic. A 2016 and a 2018 study didn't find fuller lips consistently more attractive. [11] [12] But this might be because fuller lips are only more attractive up to a point. And after crossing that point, they start becoming less attractive.

A 2023 study asked people to rate pictures of women before and after getting lip fillers. They concluded that the women with thin lips all became more attractive with fuller lips, but the group with already thick lips became less attractive after the filler. [13]

So if you have thin lips, you'll benefit from getting hyaluronic acid filler; if you already have full lips, it will probably make you less attractive.

If you want a temporary solution to get bigger lips, there are now vacuum lip plumpers that will make your lips bigger for a few hours and give you a preview of what you'll look like if you decide to get filler.

Lip gloss plumpers will also achieve a similar effect, although not as visible or long-lasting as vacuum lip plumpers.

Skin

Smooth skin is proven to make people more attractive and is believed to be a sign of health and fertility. [14] People with smooth skin are also seen as more competent and trustworthy. [15]

The 2 Most Important Skincare Products

Sunscreen – A 2013 study followed 903 adults who were asked to wear sunscreen daily. After 4 and a half years, there was no detectable increase in skin aging. This means we can delay skin aging by half a decade, and probably even more (since the study stopped after 4,5 years) by using sunscreen every day. [22]

My practical trick is to always keep a bottle of sunscreen in my purse and next to my house door. This way, whenever I'm leaving the house, I see it and apply it.

Tretinoin – A systematic review of randomized controlled trials found that tretinoin is an effective and safe way to improve wrinkles, improve skin tone, and reduce patchy and irregular skin pigmentation. [23] Check the top posts of all time in the subreddit r/tretinoin to see its phenomenal efficacy.

A viable alternative to tretinoin is Adapalene, brand name Differin, which is actually sold over the counter in the US. Although there's less research about it, one 2018 study found that it can work as well as tretinoin for anti-aging purposes. [24]

Supplements for Better Skin

Wrinkles are a sign of age, and less wrinkled skin is perceived as more attractive.

Two supplements have been shown to reduce wrinkles:

Collagen supplements – A 2022 systematic review of 12 studies concluded that oral collagen supplementation reduces wrinkles around the eyes, reduces skin roughness, and improves skin elasticity and hydration. [16] The recommended dose is 10 grams daily, but studies have shown positive effects on the skin with doses as low as 2 grams. [17]

Hyaluronic acid supplements – Three randomized controlled trials have found that oral hyaluronic acid supplements reduce wrinkles. [18] [19] [20] Don't bother with creams or anything you put directly on your skin, as it hasn't been shown to be better than a placebo. [21]

Microneedling

Microneedling, also known as collagen induction therapy, or vampire facials, is a procedure that uses tiny sterile needles to puncture the skin and rejuvenate it.

A 2018 review of the clinical evidence concluded that microneedling is a safe, effective, and minimally invasive treatment to improve many skin conditions, including acne, scars, thin wrinkle lines, and stretch marks. [25]

If you want to see how well it works, you can check before and after pictures on sites like RealSelf or reddit.

Even though most people do microneedling treatments in clinics, it's actually very cheap to own a microneedling machine. I own a Derminator 2 (once again, I'm not paid to promote this brand; it's just the one I use), which cost me around 200 dollars. I do one treatment at home once every 3 weeks. The results have been amazing, especially on my acne scars which have almost completely disappeared.

My Recommended Routine

My minimalistic and highly effective skincare routine consists only of sunscreen during the day, tretinoin at night, collagen and hyaluronic acid supplements, and one microneedling session once every three weeks. As usual, there are infinite options for skin care, but in my opinion, this approach will give you 95% or more of the results without having to invest too much time or money.

Breast Size

Even though studies have found mixed results, average or above-average breast sizes are generally considered more attractive than smaller breast sizes. [1] Waitresses with bigger breasts get bigger tips in restaurants. [2] But breast firmness might be more important than size. [3]

If you'd like to have bigger breasts, you might believe that your only option is breast implants. But there is at least one other effective way to increase breast size. And it's one I've used successfully.

Nonsurgical Breast Augmentation

Multiple studies have found that it's possible to increase breast size using negative pressure expansion devices. [4,5,6]

These devices look like cups that are placed over the breasts and create a vacuum. Over time, with the increased pressure and blood flow, the body creates new fat cells and mammary tissue, making the breasts bigger. Tissue expanders like these have been safely used for decades as a reconstructive treatment for women who had mastectomies. They're also commonly used to heal wounds, a treatment called Negative-Pressure Wound Therapy.

The first studies testing this method used modified bras that would have to be worn for 10 to 12 hours a day over several months, keeping the breasts under a vacuum pressure of 20 mmHg. But a 2022 study found that even using it for 15 minutes a day causes tissue growth. [5]

A 2007 study found that using a breast expander for an average of 4 months caused an average increase in volume of 150 cubic centimeters (cc). [6] Using it for more days was associated with more growth. The average growth seemed to be 1 to 1.5 cc a day.

For reference, the most common breast implant volume is 300 to 400 cc, which results in a 1 or 2 cups increase in bra size.

So, this was the old method. Low pressure for 10 hours a day. The recent 2022 study had women wear the vacuum cups for only 15 minutes daily but at higher pressures. Instead of 20 mmHg for 10 hours, like in the previous studies, they wore it for only 15 minutes a day with pressures of 60 mmHg or 100 mmHg.

The study lasted only a month, and the average increase was 30 cc. This meant their breasts also grew an average of 1 cc a day, similar to the previous studies, but with only 15 minutes a day instead of 10 hours!

Last year, after learning about these studies, I ordered a breast expander and started using it consistently at night. I didn't track how much pressure I used; I just increased it until I felt slightly uncomfortable and made sure to wear it for at least 15 minutes every day. After 15 minutes, I would take a break and repeat for one or more "sets."

After doing this consistently for 8 months, I'm up almost 2 cup sizes!

A recent post on the subreddit r/nbe (which stands for Natural Breast Enhancement) shows a woman who grew 4 cup sizes with a breast expander! [7]

She wore it for one hour daily, 4 sets of 12 minutes, with a 3-minute rest between sets. In the comments, she links to an older forum post where a different girl grew her breasts from a 34A to a 34DD by wearing it also for one hour a day, but without breaks, just one hour straight. [8]

After seeing both her posts and results, this is also what I'm doing now. One hour once a day, at night, while watching tv or reading. I hope to grow at least one extra cup size over the next year.

Breast Implants

Breast implants are the best option if you want faster results or to achieve a specific size or look. They're one of the most common plastic surgeries performed worldwide and have a very high satisfaction rate. In Realself, 95% of women who got the procedure thought it was worth it.

Fat Transfer to the Breasts

Instead of having implants, there's also the option of having fat transferred from other parts of the body to the breasts.

The advantages are that they'll maybe look and feel more natural. The disadvantage is that sometimes the fat doesn't stay and gets reabsorbed into the body, so some women end up dissatisfied with the results. Even though this is a risk, 88% of women in Realself rate the procedure as worth it.

Conclusion

Last night I went out to a club with some friends and had a surreal, almost out-of-body experience while dancing at the end of the night.

It suddenly hit me that I had fun the entire night. That I was feeling very happy. And I didn't even drink alcohol that night.

For a long time, every time I went out, I never really enjoyed myself. I would just feel an avalanche of "I'm not good enough, attractive enough, free enough." I would see my friends laughing, telling stories, making jokes, flirting, and even though I also tried to do it, I always felt like something was blocking me. I was too self-conscious, too different; I couldn't completely relax and be in the moment.

And last night, while dancing in the club, I had this moment where suddenly I realized that my plan worked. I was lost in my memories for a minute, remembering that night of pain when I decided that something had to change, and then my mind brought me back to the present. I felt like I suddenly time-traveled to my dream life. I had fantasized so much about that exact moment, where the fog of feeling "not good enough" wouldn't be around me anymore. And I'm finally free from it.

I don't think most people are experiencing exactly the same kind of pain I was feeling back then. I clearly had some serious self-esteem issues that improved a lot through psychotherapy. But I really believe that therapy alone wouldn't have been enough. I changed many things that objectively made me a more attractive person.

And this book is now the record of what I've learned. I hope you discovered a few ideas that will improve your life too!

Thank You

Thank you so much for purchasing my book.

You could have picked from millions of other books but you took a chance and chose this one.

So THANK YOU for getting this book and for reading it all the way to the end.

Before you go, I wanted to ask you for one small favor. **Could you please consider writing a review on the platform? Posting a review is the best and easiest way to support the work of independent authors like me.**

Your feedback will help me keep writing the kind of books that (I hope) will make our lives a bit better. It would mean a lot to me to hear from you.

Notes

Hair

1. Bereczkei, T., & Mesko, N. (2006). Hair length, facial attractiveness, personality attribution: A multiple fitness model of hairdressing. Review of psychology, 13(1), 35-42.

How to Reduce Your Waist Size

1. Bell EA, Rolls BJ. Energy density of foods affects energy intake across multiple levels of fat content in lean and obese women. Am J Clin Nutr. 2001;73(6):1010-8.

2. Duncan KH, Bacon JA, Weinsier RL. The effects of high and low energy density diets on satiety, energy intake, and eating time of obese and nonobese subjects. Am J Clin Nutr. 1983;37(5):763-7.

3. Boix-Castejón M, Herranz-López M, Pérez Gago A, et al. Hibiscus and lemon verbena polyphenols modulate appetite-related biomarkers in overweight subjects: a randomized controlled trial. Food Funct. 2018;9(6):3173-84.

4. Phung OJ, Baker WL, Matthews LJ, Lanosa M, Thorne A, Coleman CI. Effect of green tea catechins with or without caffeine on anthropometric measures: a systematic review and meta-analysis. Am J Clin Nutr. 2010;91(1):73-81.

5. Maharlouei, N., Tabrizi, R., Lankarani, K. B., Rezaianzadeh, A., Akbari, M., Kolahdooz, F., Rahimi, M., Keneshlou, F., & Asemi, Z. (2019). The effects of ginger intake on weight loss and metabolic profiles among overweight and obese subjects: A systematic review and meta-analysis of randomized controlled trials. Critical reviews in food science and nutrition, 59(11), 1753-1766.

6. Kondo T, Kishi M, Fushimi T, Ugajin S, Kaga T. Vinegar intake reduces body weight, body fat mass, and serum triglyceride levels in obese Japanese subjects. Biosci Biotechnol Biochem. 2009;73(8):1837-43.

7. Genta S, Cabrera W, Habib N, et al. Yacon syrup: beneficial effects on obesity and insulin resistance in humans. Clin Nutr. 2009;28(2):182-7.

8. Cicero A, Derosa G, Bove M, Imola F, Borghi C, Gaddi A. Psyllium improves dyslipidaemia, hyperglycaemia and hypertension, while guar gum reduces body weight more rapidly in patients affected by metabolic syndrome following an AHA Step 2 diet. Med J Nutrition Metab. 2009;3(1):47-54.

9. Corney RA, Sunderland C, James LJ. Immediate pre-meal water ingestion decreases voluntary food intake in lean young males. Eur J Nutr. 2016;55(2):815-9.

10. How I Lost 6 Inches Of My Waist - One Year Waist Slimming Exercise! - https://youtu.be/WD3h0dznep8

11. Jewell ML, Weiss RA, Baxter RA, Cox SE, Dover JS, Donofrio LM, et al. Safety and tolerability of high-intensity focused ultrasonography for noninvasive body sculpting: 24-week data from a randomized, sham-controlled study. Aesthet Surg J. 2012;32(7):868–76.

12. Fatemi A, Kane MA. High-intensity focused ultrasound effectively reduces waist circumference by ablating adipose tissue from the abdomen and flanks: a retrospective case series. Aesthetic Plast Surg. 2010;34(5):577-82.

13. Ascher B. Safety and efficacy of UltraShape Contour I treatments to improve the appearance of body contours: multiple treatments in shorter intervals. Aesthet Surg J. 2010;30(2):217-24.

14. Weiss RA. Noninvasive radio frequency for skin tightening and body contouring. Semin Cutan Med Surg. 2013;32(1):9-17.

15. Manuskiatti W, Wachirakaphan C, Lektrakul N, Varothai S. Circumference reduction and cellulite treatment with a TriPollar radiofrequency device: a pilot study. J Eur Acad Dermatol Venereol. 2009;23(7):820-7.

16. Van der Lugt C, Romero C, Ancona D, Al-Zarouni M, Perera J, Trelles MA. A multicenter study of cellulite treatment with a variable emission radio frequency system. Dermatol Ther. 2009;22(1):74-84.

17. Alexiades-Armenakas M, Dover JS, Arndt KA. Unipolar radiofrequency treatment to improve the appearance of cellulite. J Cosmet Laser Ther. 2008;10(3):148-53.

18. Wanitphakdeedecha R, Manuskiatti W. Treatment of cellulite with a bipolar radiofrequency, infrared heat, and pulsatile suction device: a pilot study. J Cosmet Dermatol. 2006;5(4):284-8.

19. Assim, Y. M., K. S. A. El-Aziz, G. E. E. Refaye, and A. T. Youssef, "Effect of ultrasound cavitation versus radiofrequency on abdominal fat thickness in postnatal women", Eurasian Journal of Biosciences, 2020.

20. Mahmoud ELdesoky, M. T., Mohamed Abutaleb, E. E., & Mohamed Mousa, G. S. (2016). Ultrasound cavitation versus cryolipolysis for non-invasive body contouring. The Australasian journal of dermatology, 57(4), 288-293. https://doi.org/10.1111/ajd.12386

21. Assim, Y. M., El-Aziz, A., Khadiga, S., EL Refaye, G. E., & Youssef, A. T. (2020). Effect of ultrasound cavitation versus radiofrequency on abdominal fat thickness in postnatal women. EurAsian Journal of BioSciences, 14(2).

22. Bani, D., Li, A. Q., Freschi, G., & Russo, G. L. (2013). Histological and ultrastructural effects of ultrasound-induced cavitation on human skin adipose tissue. Plastic and Reconstructive Surgery Global Open, 1(6).

23. Kinney, B. M., & Lozanova, P. (2019). High intensity focused electromagnetic therapy evaluated by magnetic resonance imaging: Safety and efficacy study of a dual tissue effect based non-invasive abdominal body shaping. Lasers in surgery and medicine, 51(1), 40-46. https://doi.org/10.1002/lsm.23024

24. Kent, D. E., & Jacob, C. I. (2019). Simultaneous changes in abdominal adipose and muscle tissues following treatments by high-intensity focused electromagnetic (HIFEM) technology-based device: computed tomography evaluation. J Drugs Dermatol, 18(11), 1098-1102.

25. Avci, P., Nyame, T. T., Gupta, G. K., Sadasivam, M., & Hamblin, M. R. (2013). Low-level laser therapy for fat layer reduction: a comprehensive review. Lasers in surgery and medicine, 45(6), 349-357. https://doi.org/10.1002/lsm.22153

26. Caruso-Davis, M. K., Guillot, T. S., Podichetty, V. K., Mashtalir, N., Dhurandhar, N. V., Dubuisson, O., Yu, Y., & Greenway, F. L. (2011). Efficacy of low-level laser therapy for body contouring and spot fat reduction. Obesity surgery, 21(6), 722–729. https://doi.org/10.1007/s11695-010-0126-y

27. Abdi Dezfouli, R., Hosseinpour, A., Qorbani, M., & Daneshzad, E. (2023). The efficacy of topical aminophylline in local fat reduction: A systematic review. Frontiers in endocrinology, 14, 1087614. https://doi.org/10.3389/fendo.2023.1087614

28. Caruso, M. K., Pekarovic, S., Raum, W. J., & Greenway, F. (2007). Topical fat reduction from the waist. Diabetes, obesity & metabolism, 9(3), 300–303. https://doi.org/10.1111/j.1463-1326.2006.00600.x

29. Singh, D., Dixson, B. J., Jessop, T. S., Morgan, B., & Dixson, A. F. (2010). Cross-cultural consensus for waist–hip ratio and women's attractiveness. Evolution and Human Behavior, 31(3), 176-181.

30. Marlowe, F., & Wetsman, A. (2001). Preferred waist-to-hip ratio and ecology. Personality and Individual Differences, 30(3), 481-489.

31. Karremans, J. C., Frankenhuis, W. E., & Arons, S. (2010). Blind men prefer a low waist-to-hip ratio. Evolution and Human Behavior, 31(3), 182-186.

How to Increase Your Hip Size

1. Brad J. Schoenfeld, Dan Ogborn & James W. Krieger (2017) Dose-response relationship between weekly resistance training volume and increases in muscle mass: A systematic review and meta-analysis, Journal of Sports Sciences, 35:11, 1073-1082

2. Kreider, R. B., & Stout, J. R. (2021). Creatine in Health and Disease. Nutrients, 13(2), 447. https://doi.org/10.3390/nu13020447

3. Rosqvist, F., Iggman, D., Kullberg, J., Cedernaes, J., Johansson, H. E., Larsson, A., Johansson, L., Ahlström, H., Arner, P., Dahlman, I., & Risérus, U. (2014). Overfeeding polyunsaturated and saturated fat causes distinct effects on

liver and visceral fat accumulation in humans. Diabetes, 63(7), 2356-2368. https://doi.org/10.2337/db13-1622

4. Cansancao, A. L., Condé-Green, A., Gouvea Rosique, R., Junqueira Rosique, M., & Cervantes, A. (2019). "Brazilian Butt Lift" Performed by Board-Certified Brazilian Plastic Surgeons: Reports of an Expert Opinion Survey. Plastic and reconstructive surgery, 144(3), 601-609. https://doi.org/10.1097/PRS.0000000000006020

5. Keyes GR, Singer R, Iverson RE, et al.Incidence and predictors of venous thromboembolism in abdominoplasty. Aesthet Surg J. 2018;38:162-173.

6. Lin, M. J., Dubin, D. P., & Khorasani, H. (2020). Poly-L-Lactic Acid for Minimally Invasive Gluteal Augmentation. Dermatologic surgery : official publication for American Society for Dermatologic Surgery [et al.], 46(3), 386-394. https://doi.org/10.1097/DSS.0000000000001967

7. Palm M. (2021). Magnetic Resonance Imaging Evaluation of Changes in Gluteal Muscles After Treatments With the High-Intensity Focused Electromagnetic Procedure. Dermatologic surgery : official publication for American Society for Dermatologic Surgery [et al.], 47(3), 386-391. https://doi.org/10.1097/DSS.0000000000002764

8. Plotkin, D. L., Rodas, M. A., Vigotsky, A., McIntosh, M. C., Breeze, E., Ubrik, R., ... & Roberts, M. D. (2023). Hip thrust and back squat training elicit similar gluteus muscle hypertrophy and transfer similarly to the deadlift. bioRxiv, 2023-06.

Facial Attractiveness

1. Beall A. E. (2007). Can a new smile make you look more intelligent and successful?. Dental clinics of North America, 51(2), 289-vii. https://doi.org/10.1016/j.cden.2007.02.002

2. Grosofsky, A., Adkins, S., Bastholm, R., Meyer, L., Krueger, L., Meyer, J., & Torma, P. (2003). Tooth color: effects on judgments of attractiveness and age. Perceptual and motor skills, 96(1), 43-48. https://doi.org/10.2466/pms.2003.96.1.43

3. Chaudhary, D., Patthi, B., Singla, A., Gupta, R., Muchhal, M., Kumar, J. K., ... & Dhama, K. (2018). The Anticariogenic Efficacy of 5000 ppm Fluoridated Toothpaste: A Systematic Review. Journal of Clinical & Diagnostic Research, 12(1).

4. Gendreau, L., Barlow, A. P., & Mason, S. C. (2011). Overview of the clinical evidence for the use of NovaMin in providing relief from the pain of dentin hypersensitivity. The Journal of clinical dentistry, 22(3), 90-95.

5. Ren, H., Chen, X., & Zhang, Y. (2021). Correlation between facial attractiveness and facial components assessed by laypersons and orthodontists. Journal of dental sciences, 16(1), 431-436. https://doi.org/10.1016/j.jds.2020.07.012

6. Sena, L. M. F., Damasceno E Araújo, L. A. L., Farias, A. C. R., & Pereira, H. S. G. (2017). The influence of sagittal position of the mandible in facial attractiveness and social perception. Dental press journal of orthodontics, 22(2), 77-86. https://doi.org/10.1590/2177-6709.22.2.077-086.oar

7. Naini, F. B., Donaldson, A. N., McDonald, F., & Cobourne, M. T. (2012). Assessing the influence of chin prominence on perceived attractiveness in the orthognathic patient, clinician and layperson. International journal of oral and maxillofacial surgery, 41(7), 839-846. https://doi.org/10.1016/j.ijom.2012.01.012

8. Przylipiak, M., Przylipiak, J., Terlikowski, R., Lubowicka, E., Chrostek, L., & Przylipiak, A. (2018). Impact of face proportions on face attractiveness. Journal of Cosmetic Dermatology. doi:10.1111/jocd.12783

9. Parsa, K. M., Charipova, K., Coerdt, K., Clark, C. M., Wang, H., Chu, E., & Reilly, M. J. (2021). The Role of Age and Gender on Perception of Women After Cosmetic Rhinoplasty. Aesthetic plastic surgery, 45(3), 1184-1190. https://doi.org/10.1007/s00266-020-02030-4

10. Stephen, I. D., & McKeegan, A. M. (2010). Lip colour affects perceived sex typicality and attractiveness of human faces. Perception, 39(8), 1104-1110. https://doi.org/10.1068/p6730

11. Heidekrueger, P. I., Szpalski, C., Weichman, K., Juran, S., Ng, R., Claussen, C., Ninkovic, M., & Broer, P. N. (2017). Lip Attractiveness: A Cross-Cultural Analysis. Aesthetic surgery journal, 37(7), 828-836. https://doi.org/10.1093/asj/sjw168

12. Przylipiak, M., Przylipiak, J., Terlikowski, R., Lubowicka, E., Chrostek, L., & Przylipiak, A. (2018). Impact of face proportions on face attractiveness. Journal of cosmetic dermatology, 17(6), 954-959. https://doi.org/10.1111/jocd.12783

13. de Queiroz Hernandez, P. M., Cotrin, P., Valarelli, F. P., de Oliveira, R. C. G., Bispo, C. G. C., Freitas, K. M. S., ... & Cotrin, D. P. (2023). Evaluation of the attractiveness of lips with different volumes after filling with hyaluronic acid. Scientific Reports, 13(1), 4589.

14. Fink, B., Grammer, K., & Thornhill, R. (2001). Human (Homo sapiens) facial attractiveness in relation to skin texture and color. Journal of comparative psychology (Washington, D.C. : 1983), 115(1), 92-99. https://doi.org/10.1037/0735-7036.115.1.92

15. Tsankova, E., & Kappas, A. (2016). Facial Skin Smoothness as an Indicator of Perceived Trustworthiness and Related Traits. Perception, 45(4), 400-408. https://doi.org/10.1177/0301006615616748

16. Al-Atif H. (2022). Collagen Supplements for Aging and Wrinkles: A Paradigm Shift in the Fields of Dermatology and Cosmetics. Dermatology practical & conceptual, 12(1), e2022018. https://doi.org/10.5826/dpc.1201a18

17. Kim, J., Lee, S. G., Lee, J., Choi, S., Suk, J., Lee, J. H., Yang, J. H., Yang, J. S., & Kim, J. (2022). Oral Supplementation of Low-Molecular-Weight Collagen Peptides Reduces Skin Wrinkles and Improves Biophysical Properties of Skin: A Randomized, Double-Blinded, Placebo-Controlled Study. Journal of medicinal food, 25(12), 1146-1154. https://doi.org/10.1089/jmf.2022.K.0097

18. Michelotti, A., Cestone, E., De Ponti, I., Pisati, M., Sparta, E., & Tursi, F. (2021). Oral intake of a new full-spectrum hyaluronan improves skin profilometry and ageing: a randomized, double-blind, placebo-controlled clinical trial. European journal of dermatology : EJD, 31(6), 798-805. https://doi.org/10.1684/ejd.2021.4176

19. Oe, M., Sakai, S., Yoshida, H., Okado, N., Kaneda, H., Masuda, Y., & Urushibata, O. (2017). Oral hyaluronan relieves wrinkles: a double-blinded, placebo-controlled study over a 12-week period. Clinical, cosmetic and investigational dermatology, 10, 267–273. https://doi.org/10.2147/CCID.S141845

20. Hsu, T. F., Su, Z. R., Hsieh, Y. H., Wang, M. F., Oe, M., Matsuoka, R., & Masuda, Y. (2021). Oral Hyaluronan Relieves Wrinkles and Improves Dry Skin: A 12-Week Double-Blinded, Placebo-Controlled Study. Nutrients, 13(7), 2220. https://doi.org/10.3390/nu13072220

21. Boen, M., Alhaddad, M., Wu, D. C., & Goldman, M. P. (2020). A Prospective Double-blind, Placebo-controlled Clinical Trial Evaluating the Efficacy of a Novel Combination of Hyaluronic Acid Serum and Antioxidant Cream for Rejuvenation of the Aging Neck. The Journal of clinical and aesthetic dermatology, 13(11), 13–18.

22. Hughes, M. C., Williams, G. M., Baker, P., & Green, A. C. (2013). Sunscreen and prevention of skin aging: a randomized trial. Annals of internal medicine, 158(11), 781–790. https://doi.org/10.7326/0003-4819-158-11-201306040-00002

23. Sitohang, I. B. S., Makes, W. I., Sandora, N., & Suryanegara, J. (2022). Topical tretinoin for treating photoaging: A systematic review of randomized controlled trials. International journal of women's dermatology, 8(1), e003. https://doi.org/10.1097/JW9.0000000000000003

24. Bagatin, E., Gonçalves, H. S., Sato, M., Almeida, L. M. C., & Miot, H. A. (2018). Comparable efficacy of adapalene 0.3% gel and tretinoin 0.05% cream as treatment for cutaneous photoaging. European journal of dermatology : EJD, 28(3), 343–350. https://doi.org/10.1684/ejd.2018.3320

25. Alster, T. S., & Graham, P. M. (2018). Microneedling: a review and practical guide. Dermatologic Surgery, 44(3), 397-404.

Breast Size

1. Zelazniewicz, A. M., & Pawlowski, B. (2011). Female breast size attractiveness for men as a function of sociosexual orientation (restricted vs. unrestricted). Archives of Sexual Behavior, 40, 1129-1135.

2. Lynn, M. (2009). Determinants and consequences of female attractiveness and sexiness: Realistic tests with restaurant waitresses. Archives of sexual Behavior, 38, 737-745.

3. Koscinski K. (2019). Breast firmness is of greater importance for women's attractiveness than breast size. American journal of human biology : the official journal of the Human Biology Council, 31(5), e23287. https://doi.org/10.1002/ajhb.23287

4. Khouri, R. K., Schlenz, I., Murphy, B. J., & Baker, T. J. (2000). Nonsurgical breast enlargement using an external soft-tissue expansion system. Plastic and reconstructive surgery, 105(7), 2500–2514. https://doi.org/10.1097/00006534-200006000-00032

5. Oh, J., Kim, M., Oh, J., & Heo, C. Y. (2022). Efficacy of breast augmentation using an external breast tissue expander for a shorter period while applying higher pressure: a preliminary study. Archives of Aesthetic Plastic Surgery, 28(1), 9-16.

6. Schlenz, I., & Kaider, A. (2007). The Brava external tissue expander: is breast enlargement without surgery a reality?. Plastic and reconstructive surgery, 120(6), 1680–1689. https://doi.org/10.1097/01.prs.0000267637.43207.19

7. https://www.reddit.com/r/nbe/comments/13jkci9/

8. https://forum.noogleberry.com/index.php?threads/finally-hit-the-2-year-mark.4306/

www.ingramcontent.com/pod-product-compliance
Lightning Source LLC
LaVergne TN
LVHW061615070526
838199LV00078B/7287